the Bookery Cook

ART TO EAT

JESSICA THOMPSON   GEORGIA THOMPSON   MAXINE THOMPSON

MURDOCH BOOKS

For Mum and Dad, and the art of sharing food.

Contents

Foreword

by King Adz

I was chuffed to bits when I got an email from three Australian sisters who had been developing their own idea for a wicked cookbook, and had been inspired by my first foray into food writing — *The Urban Cookbook* — to get their own book out there. As you are now holding it in your hands, either reading it in the shop or having made a very wise decision and invested in it, you will find that this book is seriously original and I am very proud to be involved.

Food and creativity is a powerful combination. Is food art? Probably. But what I like most about creative cooking is that you are producing something that can be almost instantly appreciated. Good food stays around for a lot less time than even the most transient street art, which is considered ephemeral. Good tucker is only around for a fleeting moment, before someone snaffles it up and asks for more.

My favourite place in my house is the kitchen, and once I'm there cooking I can travel around the world in a lot less than eighty days (without leaving the comfort of my own home). This book is not only a journey into food and art, it's also a travel guide for your taste buds. With over a hundred recipes, it will have you bouncing around the globe, no matter where you are cooking.

Much of my time is spent cooking and writing about street food, which I consider to be the freshest form of cuisine. For the past twenty years I have travelled from country to country discovering and writing about street culture, and it is on those streets that I've had the pleasure to eat. The thing about food that I love the most, is that it unites everyone in the world. We all have to eat, no matter what race, religion or gender. Food is a good place to start if you want to help spread a bit of peace and love — a theme that is very important for the world right now.

Some of the recipes and art in this book are influenced by experiences 'on the street' and this is indeed a mark of quality for me — a badge of honour. So without further ado, I raise my glass of Rwandan Shandy (Coke and Guinness, discovered on a trip to Kigali) to *The Bookery Cook*.

Introduction

Food and art

It's hard to pin-point exactly when our infatuation with food began. From breaking into kitchen cupboards when we were toddlers, pulling out any foodstuffs we could reach to empty on the floor to make 'pancakes', to building campfires in our backyard to make doughy burnt damper, cooking and entertaining has always been something that has come naturally. Mornings are spent discussing breakfast, lunch and dinner options – a friend once said that we are the only people she knew who talked about dinner before they'd finished breakfast.

Hungry for a new adventure in our early twenties, we moved to Bristol in the UK, where we were inspired by the new cultures and food experiences that come with living so close to Europe – pizza in Napoli, habas con Jamon in Spain, bastilla in Morocco and jerk chicken cooked in drum barrels in the UK. We worked in pubs and restaurants, travelled when we could, cooked for new friends, and started to collect our recipes.

Eventually all making our way back home (Jessie later, via a year in Japan), we took up residence together. Again, cooking and entertaining was the heart of our house – friends would knock on our door on a Friday evening or Sunday afternoon knowing that something would be brewing. Guests were always ready and willing to get involved by kneading dough, rolling pasta, grinding peppercorns, shelling pistachios, choosing music or pouring wine. We started The Bookery Cook blog and book around this time, wanting to share our recipes and love for food.

The idea of a collaboratively illustrated cookbook came about during a dinner one night with about 20 friends. As the evening progressed, someone pulled out pens and paper and we all started drawing what we'd eaten. Some sketches were literal representations of food, some more abstract. Inspired by this idea, we approached artists and designers all over the world to produce artworks to accompany the recipes in the book. We are lucky to have met such an incredible and talented range of people who have helped bring this book to life – lifting the recipes off the pages and into the imagination.

The recipes in this book emphasise soulful, balanced meals from many global cuisines. Some recipes are quick and straightforward, others more challenging – but all are designed to be accessible, tasty and made for sharing.

Now living in different places, our love for food keeps us close – messages about a new dining hotspot, pictures of produce, a quick phone call about a recipe, and other edible moments.

Breakfasts

Mornings can be distinctively sweet or savoury, made up of Vegemite or jam on toast, baked pancetta egg cups or ricotta hotcakes. This chapter provides a variety of breakfast options ranging from the healthy to the more indulgent, with ideas for different occasions and preparation times.

Smoked salmon scrambled eggs with dill, caper and onion salsa

A deliciously Scandinavian-style start to the day, this breakfast combines smoked fish, creamy eggs and a salsa of fresh dill and salty capers. The salsa also goes well with boiled or poached eggs, steamed and grilled fish, and all manner of potatoes.

PREPARATION TIME: 20 MINUTES
COOKING TIME: 5 MINUTES
SERVES: 4

8 eggs
125 ml (4 fl oz/½ cup) pouring (whipping) cream
200 g (7 oz) smoked salmon, sliced into thin strips
30 g (1 oz) butter
4 slices sourdough bread, lightly toasted, to serve
lemon wedges, to serve

DILL, CAPER AND ONION SALSA
½ large onion, finely chopped
2 tablespoons capers, rinsed and finely chopped
2 tablespoons finely chopped fresh dill
2 teaspoons lemon juice
2 teaspoons olive oil

To make the dill, caper and onion salsa, combine all of the ingredients in a bowl and set aside.

Whisk together the eggs and cream in a bowl. Add the smoked salmon and season with freshly ground black pepper.

Melt the butter in a frying pan over medium–low heat and add the egg mixture. Use a wooden spoon or spatula to push the eggs from the base of the pan as they start to set and try to avoid overworking them — this will keep the eggs smooth and glossy. Cook the eggs for about 3 minutes, or until set. Remove the pan from the heat and season with sea salt.

Serve the scrambled eggs with the salsa and a wedge of lemon.

Artwork by
Femke de Jong
digital illustration

BREAKFAST MUSHROOMS

Citrus roasted mushrooms on sourdough

Cooked with a citrus twist, these fairy-tale favourites will bring a touch of psychedelia to your morning!

PREPARATION TIME: 10 MINUTES
COOKING TIME: 20 MINUTES
SERVES: 2

1 tablespoon olive oil
20 g (¾ oz) butter, cubed, plus extra to serve
1 garlic clove, finely chopped
2 tablespoons roughly chopped flat-leaf (Italian) parsley
1 teaspoon roughly chopped thyme
1 teaspoon finely grated lemon zest
2 tablespoons lemon juice
300 g (10½ oz) field mushrooms, roughly chopped
½ teaspoon sea salt
½ teaspoon freshly ground black pepper
2 slices sourdough bread, lightly toasted, to serve

Preheat the oven to 180°C (350°F/Gas 4). Combine all of the ingredients, except for the bread, in a bowl and mix well to coat the mushrooms in the flavourings. Line a baking tray with a large sheet of foil and place the mushroom mixture in the centre, then pull the edges of the foil together and seal to make a parcel.

Roast the mushroom parcel in the oven for 20 minutes, or until the mushrooms have softened. Pile the roasted mushrooms on hot buttered toast, season with salt and pepper and devour immediately!

Artwork by
Belinda Suzette
watercolour and digital media

Leg ham, gruyère and brioche toastie

Not just your ordinary ham and cheese toasted sandwich, this classy version boasts gruyère cheese, ham off the bone and brioche bread — perfect if the French aristocracy were to drop in for brunch. If you go to the effort of making your own brioche you won't regret it, especially when you pull the warm, golden, buttery loaf from the oven. If you don't have the time you can use a loaf from your local bakery.

PREPARATION TIME: 15 MINUTES + 5 HOURS FOR BRIOCHE
COOKING TIME: 10 MINUTES + 40 MINUTES FOR BRIOCHE
SERVES: 2

20 g (¾ oz) butter
4 slices brioche, preferably homemade (see right)
2 teaspoons mustard
6 slices leg ham off the bone
4 slices gruyère cheese

BRIOCHE

300 g (10½ oz/2 cups) plain (all-purpose) flour
7 g (¼ oz/2 teaspoons) active dried yeast
2 tablespoons caster (superfine) sugar
150 g (5½ oz) butter, softened
3 eggs, plus 1 egg yolk extra for glazing
a pinch of salt
80 ml (2½ fl oz/⅓ cup) milk, at room temperature

To make the brioche, combine all of the ingredients, except for the milk, in a large bowl. Turn out onto a lightly floured work surface and knead until smooth, about 10 minutes by hand or 6 minutes if you are using an electric mixer fitted with a dough hook attachment. Place the dough in a lightly greased bowl, cover with a clean damp tea towel (dish towel), and leave to rise in a warm place until doubled in size, about 3 hours.

Lightly grease a 1.25 litre (44 fl oz/5 cup) capacity brioche tin. Punch down the dough, then add 3 tablespoons of the milk and knead until evenly combined. Place into the prepared tin and set aside in a warm place for 1 hour to rise.

CONTINUED ➤➤

Artwork by
Fanny Dolhain
digital illustration

Preheat the oven to 200°C (400°F/Gas 6). Whisk together the remaining milk and egg yolk in a bowl and use the mixture to brush the top of the brioche. Bake in the oven for 40 minutes, or until golden brown. Remove from the oven and allow to cool for 10 minutes, before turning out onto a wire rack to cool completely. Cut into slices as needed.

To assemble the leg ham and gruyère toasties, butter one side of each slice of brioche liberally — this will be the outside of the toastie. On the other side, spread a thin layer of mustard. Layer the ham and cheese on the mustard, then top with the remaining slices, butter side outwards, and press together. Heat a large frying pan over medium heat. Place the toasties in the pan, reduce the heat to medium–low and cook for a few minutes on each side, or until the cheese has melted and the brioche is golden brown. Remove from the pan and serve hot.

Pumpkin bread with homemade ricotta

Turn the leftover pumpkin quarters hanging around your kitchen into a piping hot, sweet loaf of bread. Making your own ricotta is surprisingly simple, quick and highly addictive. If you don't have any muslin you can use a tea towel.

PREPARATION TIME: 45 MINUTES + 2 HOURS STANDING
 + 15 MINUTES DRAINING FOR HOMEMADE RICOTTA
COOKING TIME: 1 HOUR 10 MINUTES
SERVES: 4–6

PUMPKIN BREAD
300 g (10½ oz) pumpkin (winter squash), peeled, seeded and cut into 2 cm (¾ inch) cubes
300 g (10½ oz/2 cups) plain (all-purpose) flour
1 tablespoon baking powder
½ teaspoon freshly grated nutmeg
½ teaspoon ground cinnamon
½ teaspoon salt
50 g (1¾ oz) butter, softened
2 tablespoons soft brown sugar
1 egg
milk, for brushing

HOMEMADE RICOTTA
1.25 litres (44 fl oz/5 cups) milk
a pinch of salt
2 tablespoons white vinegar

To make the pumpkin bread, preheat the oven to 200°C (400°F/Gas 6). Lightly grease an 11 x 22 x 7 cm (4¼ x 8½ x 2¾ inch) loaf (bar) tin and line the base with baking paper. Place the pumpkin in a steamer over boiling water, cover and steam for about 10 minutes, or until just cooked. Transfer to a baking tray and bake in the oven for 10 minutes to dry out any excess moisture. Allow the pumpkin to cool, then mash well and set aside.

CONTINUED →→

In a bowl, sift together the flour, baking powder, spices and salt. In a separate bowl, cream together the butter and sugar using electric beaters until light and fluffy. Add the egg and beat until creamy. Stir in the flour mixture and mashed pumpkin and bring the dough together using your hands. Turn the dough out onto a lightly floured work surface and knead gently until smooth, adding a little extra flour if the dough is too sticky. Shape into a rectangle and place the dough in the prepared tin. Brush the top with milk and bake for 40 minutes, or until the loaf is golden and sounds hollow when tapped on the base.

To make homemade ricotta, rinse the inside of the saucepan you intend to use with cold water (this helps prevent the milk from burning). Place the milk in a large, heavy-based saucepan over medium heat. Add the salt and stir briefly. Allow the milk to heat up slowly, stirring occasionally. Continue to heat until you can see steam and tiny bubbles appearing on the milk (about 180°C/350°F). Remove from the heat and gently stir in the vinegar — you will notice curds start to form immediately. Cover with a clean dry tea towel (dish towel) and allow the mixture to sit undisturbed for at least 2 hours.

Take a piece of muslin (cheesecloth), dampen it slightly and place it inside a colander. With a slotted spoon, ladle out the ricotta curd into the prepared colander. Place the colander filled with the ricotta over a large bowl so it can drain freely. Let it drain for 15–60 minutes, depending on how creamy or dry you want your cheese to be. You can refrigerate for a few days (although ours never lasts that long).

To serve, spread a generous dollop of ricotta onto a slice of plain or toasted pumpkin bread. For a sweet version, drizzle the ricotta with honey and sprinkle with ground cinnamon.

Artwork by
Hayato Yoshinari
spray paint

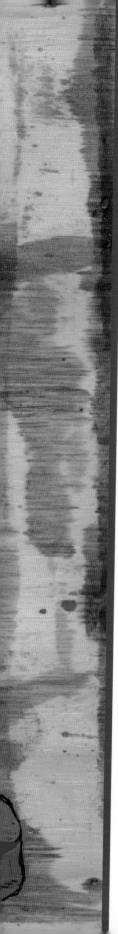

Potato cakes with poached eggs and chorizo and spinach fry

Soft potato cakes, salty chorizo, sweet wilted greens and perfectly poached eggs make for a hearty but healthy breakfast.

PREPARATION TIME: 20 MINUTES + 10 MINUTES REFRIGERATION
COOKING TIME: 35 MINUTES
SERVES: 4

POTATO CAKES
500 g (1 lb 2 oz) all-purpose
    potatoes, such as desiree, washed
20 g (¾ oz) butter
1 tablespoon milk
½ brown onion, grated
2 tablespoons finely chopped flat-
    leaf (Italian) parsley
1 egg, lightly beaten
2 tablespoons plain (all-purpose)
    flour
butter or olive oil, for frying

CHORIZO AND SPINACH FRY
2 chorizo, thinly sliced on
    the diagonal
1 garlic clove, thinly sliced
400 g (14 oz/8 cups) baby
    English spinach

POACHED EGGS
4 eggs
1 teaspoon white vinegar

To make the potato cakes, cut half of the potatoes into quarters, add to a saucepan of boiling water and cook until soft. Drain well, mash and allow to cool. Grate the remaining potatoes, squeezing out any excess liquid. Combine the mashed and grated potato in a bowl with the butter, milk, onion, parsley, egg and flour. Season with sea salt and freshly ground black pepper and mix well. Shape the potato mixture into four even-sized patties and refrigerate for at least 10 minutes to firm. Heat the butter or olive oil in a frying pan over medium heat. Add the patties, reduce the heat to medium–low and cook for 3–5 minutes on each side, or until golden and cooked through. You can keep these warm in a low oven.

To make the chorizo and spinach fry, heat a frying pan over medium heat. Add the chorizo and garlic and cook for a few minutes, stirring until the chorizo has browned on both sides. Remove from the heat, toss through the spinach until slightly wilted and transfer to a plate.

To make the poached eggs, fill a saucepan about two-thirds with water, add the vinegar and bring to a gentle boil. Crack an egg into a cup. Swirl the water in the saucepan with a spoon to create a whirlpool. Slide the egg into the centre of the whirlpool. Add additional eggs in the same way. Increase the heat if necessary to keep the water boiling gently. Cook for a few minutes until the eggs are cooked to your liking. Remove the eggs using a slotted spoon and drain. Trim any stray egg white.

To serve, stack a potato cake on top of some chorizo and spinach fry, then top each stack with an egg and season to taste.

Artwork by
Josh Rufford
mixed media on wood

Homemade baked beans

*While this recipe does cut corners in the 'bakedness' and the 'beans'
(no oven-baking required, no soaking beans overnight), it is 'homemade'
and very tasty nonetheless.*

PREPARATION TIME: 10 MINUTES
COOKING TIME: 45 MINUTES
SERVES: 4

2 tablespoons olive oil
1 brown onion, finely chopped
1 garlic clove, finely chopped
1 teaspoon smoked paprika
1½ teaspoons dijon mustard
400 g (14 oz) tin whole tomatoes,
    roughly chopped
1 teaspoon soft brown sugar
1 thyme sprig
4 whole cloves
2 x 400 g (14 oz) tin cannellini beans,
    rinsed and drained
4 slices bread, lightly toasted, to serve

Heat the olive oil in a saucepan over medium–low heat. Add the onion and garlic and cook until softened, about 8 minutes. Add the paprika and cook for a further minute, then mix in the mustard. Add the tomatoes, sugar, thyme and cloves and continue to cook for 15 minutes.

Add the cannellini beans to the pan with 125 ml (4 fl oz/½ cup) water. Reduce the heat to low, cover, and simmer for a further 20 minutes. Season with sea salt and freshly ground black pepper, to taste.

Serve the beans piled on a slice of toast or alongside your other breakfast favourites.

Artwork by
Numskull
digital illustration

'OCHAZUKE' — PRINTERS INK ON 100% RECYCLED PAPER — 1/1

Ochazuke

'Ochazuke' is a light Japanese porridge-style dish that can be quickly prepared for breakfast, or for a snack at any time of the day. It is easy to make and is a good way to use up leftover rice. Simply fill a bowl with rice, customise it with toppings, such as flaked salmon and sesame seeds, and pour over freshly brewed green tea. In Japanese, 'o' is the honorific prefix, 'cha' means tea, and 'zuke' translates to submerge.

PREPARATION TIME: 10 MINUTES
COOKING TIME: 25 MINUTES
SERVES: 2

100 g (31/2 oz/½ cup) short-grain white or brown rice, cooked (see method, page 92)
500 ml (17 fl oz/2 cups) Japanese green tea, freshly brewed from leaves is best

TOPPINGS

nori flakes (toasted seaweed) or wakame (dried seaweed)
tinned salmon or tuna, flaked
sesame seeds
bonito flakes
arare (Japanese rice cracker) or other rice crackers, broken into pieces
pickled plum
pickled ginger
tsukemono (pickled vegetables)
boiled egg
edamame
soy sauce

Divide the cooked rice between two serving bowls and top with your desired additions. If you are using nori flakes reserve these until last.

Pour over the hot green tea, sprinkle with nori and season with a little soy sauce or sea salt to taste.

To eat, slurp up the rice and toppings with chopsticks and then drink up the goodness.

Artwork by
Emily Devers
woodblock print

Baked pancetta egg cups with roasted roma tomatoes

This recipe was a menu favourite at the seaside café where Maxie did her first stint running a kitchen. These crispy, salty, perfectly formed cups will impress your breakfast companions — and they'll never guess how simple they are to make!

PREPARATION TIME: 15 MINUTES + COOLING TIME
COOKING TIME: 40 MINUTES
SERVES: 4

8 strips thinly sliced pancetta
8 eggs
2 chives, finely snipped

ROASTED TOMATOES
4 roma (plum) tomatoes, halved
2 garlic cloves, quartered
15 g (½ oz/¼ cup) finely chopped basil leaves
1 tablespoon olive oil, plus extra for greasing

To make the roasted tomatoes, preheat the oven to 180°C (350°F/Gas 4). Place the tomatoes on a baking tray, cut side up. Insert a garlic quarter and some basil into each tomato half, drizzle with olive oil and season with sea salt and freshly ground black pepper. Roast in the oven for 30–40 minutes, or until the tomatoes have softened and browned a little around the edges.

Meanwhile, make the baked pancetta egg cups. Grease 8 holes of a 125 ml (4 fl oz/ ½ cup) capacity muffin tin. Line each hole with pancetta strips to create sealed 'cups'. Bake in the oven for 5 minutes. Remove from the oven and allow to cool to room temperature.

Crack an egg into the centre of each cup and return to the oven for 2–5 minutes, or until the eggs are cooked to your liking (about 2–3 minutes for soft yolks or 4–5 minutes for firm yolks). Carefully remove the cups from the muffin tray, sprinkle with chives and season with sea salt and freshly ground black pepper.

Serve the baked pancetta egg cups with the roasted roma tomatoes alongside.

Artwork by
Georgia Thompson
digital illustration

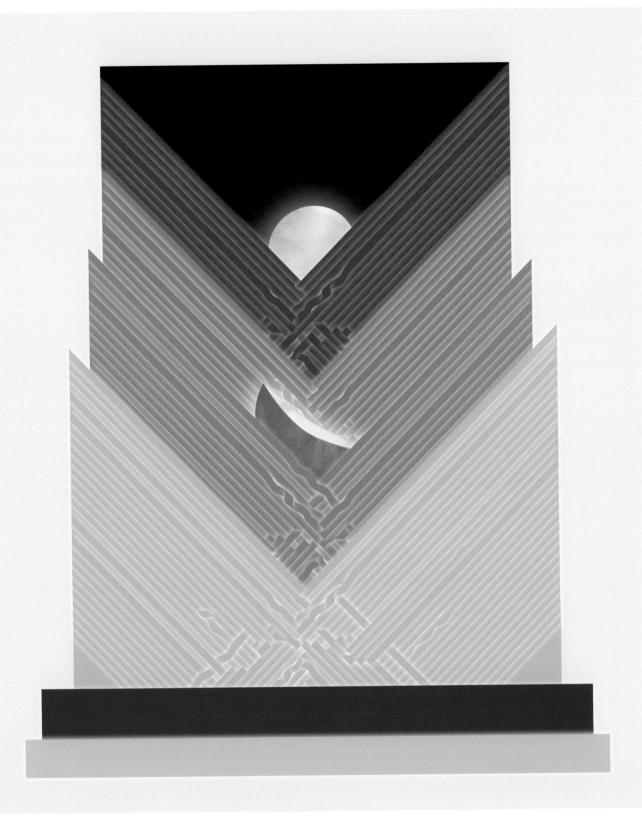

CINNAMONOMNOMNOMAPPLAIT VALLEY

Cinnamonapplait

Cinnamon + juicy apples + plaited pastry = 'cinnamonapplait'. These delicious breakfast pastries can be teamed with freshly brewed coffee for a Parisian-style breakfast.

PREPARATION TIME: 40 MINUTES
COOKING TIME: 40 MINUTES
MAKES: 8

- 2 small apples
- ½ lemon
- 75 g (2¾ oz) butter, softened
- 75 g (2¾ oz/⅓ cup) caster (superfine) sugar
- 80 g (2¾ oz/¾ cup) almond meal
- 1 egg, plus 1 egg yolk extra for glazing
- 1 tablespoon plain (all-purpose) flour
- 2 teaspoons ground cinnamon
- 1 tablespoon natural vanilla extract
- 4 sheets frozen puff pastry, defrosted

Preheat the oven to 180°C (350°F/Gas 4). Lightly grease a large baking tray. Cut the apples into quarters, removing the cores. Cut each quarter into 3 mm (⅛ inch) thick slices, squeeze over a little lemon juice and set aside.

To make the filling, cream the butter, sugar and almond meal in a bowl using electric beaters until light and fluffy. Add the egg and beat well to combine. Mix in the flour, cinnamon and vanilla extract and set aside.

Cut each sheet of puff pastry in half to make eight 20 x 12 cm (8 x 4½ inch) rectangles. Lay the rectangles lengthways on a clean work surface. Make four evenly spaced horizontal cuts on both short ends of the rectangles, about 6 cm (2½ inches) long — these strips will be used to plait the pastry. Spread about 2 tablespoons of the filling in the middle of each rectangle, about 5 cm (2 inches) wide, leaving a 1.5 cm (⅝ inch) gap at the top and bottom (so the filling doesn't ooze out and burn while cooking).

Arrange 8 apple slices on the diagonal from each edge of the filling, overlapping slightly in the centre. Plait the pastry over the apple slices by alternately folding over strips from the left and right sides. Repeat this process to make eight plaited pastries. Arrange the pastries on the prepared tray.

In a small bowl, whisk together the extra egg yolk with 1 teaspoon water. Brush over the top of the pastries and bake in the oven for 35–40 minutes, or until golden brown.

Artwork by
Thembi Hanify
digital illustration

Teepee royale

Set up camp on your breakfast plate with this novelty asparagus teepee.
For a 'teepee benedict' use ham instead of salmon.

PREPARATION TIME: 10 MINUTES
COOKING TIME: 15 MINUTES
SERVES: 2

20 g (¾ oz) butter
1 teaspoon olive oil
6 asparagus spears, trimmed
juice of ½ lime
100 g (3½ oz) smoked salmon
2 slices rye bread, lightly toasted, to serve
4 poached eggs (page 13), to serve
2 chives, finely snipped, plus 2 whole chives extra to serve

LEMONY SAUCE
2 tablespoons whole egg mayonnaise
1 tablespoon olive oil
1 tablespoon lemon juice
1 teaspoon finely chopped dill

To make the lemony sauce, whisk together the mayonnaise, olive oil, lemon juice and dill in a bowl. Season with sea salt and freshly ground black pepper and set aside.

Heat the butter and olive oil in a frying pan over medium heat. Add the asparagus and cook for about 5 minutes, turning occasionally — you want the asparagus to still be quite crunchy. When they're just about done, add the lime juice and season well with sea salt and freshly ground black pepper. Remove the pan from the heat.

To assemble the teepee, divide the smoked salmon between the slices of toast and top each with two poached eggs. Drizzle over the lemony sauce and sprinkle with the snipped chives. Construct a teepee using 3 asparagus spears with the heads pointing upwards and use a whole chive to tie the heads together.

Artwork by
Rachael Bartram
pencil on paper

Dark chocolate toastie with Cointreau dipping cream

For the serious sweet tooth, when French toast or hotcakes aren't cutting it, this sinful bittersweet toastie is bound to hit the spot. We recommend chocolate with about 60 per cent cocoa solids, and you can sprinkle a little sea salt over the chocolate to make it (even more) moreish.

PREPARATION TIME: 10 MINUTES
COOKING TIME: 10 MINUTES
SERVES: 2

40 g (1½ oz) butter
4 thick slices white bread
100 g (3½ oz/⅔ cup) dark chocolate melts (buttons)
125 ml (4 fl oz/½ cup) pouring (whipping) cream
1 tablespoon Cointreau

Butter the bread slices on one side. Use the bread to make a sandwich filled with chocolate melts, with the buttered sides facing outwards. Cook the toasties in a frying pan over low heat — this is important as you need to ensure that the chocolate melts. Increase the heat until the bread is golden, then set aside.

In a separate bowl, whisk together the cream and Cointreau. Transfer to small individual bowls to serve.

To serve, cut each toastie in half and serve immediately with the Cointreau cream on the side, for dipping decadance.

Artwork by
Arran Gregory
pen on paper

French toast with sweet ricotta and berries

Making French toast is a great way to treat someone special, and to use up old bread. If you have leftover brioche (pages 6–8) this would work a treat.

PREPARATION TIME: 10 MINUTES
COOKING TIME: 15 MINUTES
SERVES: 4

4 eggs
125 ml (4 fl oz/½ cup) milk
½ teaspoon ground cinnamon
8 thick slices bread, such as brioche
butter, for cooking
250 g (9 oz/2 cups) fresh or frozen berries, to serve

SWEET RICOTTA
250 g (9 oz) bought or homemade ricotta (pages 9–11)
2 tablespoons honey, warmed, plus extra to serve

To make the sweet ricotta, whisk together the ricotta and honey in a small bowl until smooth and fluffy. Refrigerate until ready to serve.

To make the French toast, whisk together the eggs, milk and cinnamon in a bowl. Soak each piece of bread in the egg mixture for 1 minute on each side, then hold over the bowl to drain and set aside on a plate.

Heat a little butter in a frying pan over medium–high heat and cook the bread for about 1–2 minutes on each side, or until golden. Repeat with the remaining soaked bread slices.

To serve, arrange the French toast on serving plates and top with a generous dollop of sweet ricotta, a handful of berries and drizzle with warm honey.

Artwork by
Helen Schroeder
watercolour on paper

Fruit and nut bread

Once you've tasted this sweet and succulent loaf you're bound to wake up craving a buttery slice every morning. It is also perfect with a cup of tea any time of day. For a more savoury twist, smear it with goat's cheese or top it with slices of cheddar.

PREPARATION TIME: 40 MINUTES + 1½–2 HOURS PROVING
  + 30 MINUTES RISING
COOKING TIME: 40 MINUTES
SERVES: 6–8

> 7 g (¼ oz/2 teaspoons) active dried yeast
> 500 g (1 lb 2 oz/3⅓ cups) plain (all-purpose) flour
> ½ teaspoon salt
> 1 tablespoon finely grated orange zest
> 75 g (2¾ oz/½ cup) finely chopped dried apricots
> 95 g (3¼ oz/½ cup) finely chopped dried figs
> 80 g (2¾ oz/½ cup) finely chopped dried dates
> 60 g (2¼ oz/½ cup) finely chopped walnuts

Put the yeast in a small bowl with 330 ml (11¼ fl oz/1⅓ cups) lukewarm water and whisk to dissolve the yeast. Set aside until the liquid starts to froth, about 10 minutes.

Combine the flour, salt and orange zest in a large bowl and stir in the yeast mixture. Turn out onto a lightly floured work surface and knead for about 10 minutes, or until the dough is smooth and elastic. Place in a lightly greased bowl, cover with a clean damp tea towel (dish towel) and set aside in a warm place to rise for 1½–2 hours, or until doubled in size.

Preheat the oven to 200°C (400°F/Gas 6). Grease an 11 x 22 x 7 cm (4¼ x 8½ x 2¾ inch) loaf (bar) tin. Punch down the dough to its original size, then gently knead again for a few minutes on a lightly floured work surface. Press the dough out to make a disc about 1 cm (½ inch) thick. Scatter over the fruit and nuts and knead to evenly distribute them. Bring the dough together to form a rectangle that will fit into the prepared tin. Cover with a clean damp tea towel and set aside once more to rise for 30 minutes, or until the dough has doubled in size.

Bake the fruit loaf in the oven for 30–40 minutes, or until the loaf sounds hollow when tapped on the base. If it is browning too fast, cover the top with foil. Remove from the oven and allow to cool in the tin for 5 minutes before turning out onto a wire rack to cool completely.

Artwork by
Max Berry
acrylic on paper

Ricotta orange hotcakes with orange syrup

The addition of ricotta makes these hotcakes lighter and fluffier than their traditional counterpart. Served with creamy yoghurt and sweet, tangy citrus syrup, you'll be mopping up every last drop ...

PREPARATION TIME: 20 MINUTES
COOKING TIME: 40 MINUTES
MAKES: 10

2 eggs, separated
75 g (2¾ oz/⅓ cup) caster (superfine) sugar
230 g (8½ oz/1 cup) homemade ricotta (pages 9–11)
185 ml (6 fl oz/¾ cup) milk
1 teaspoon finely grated orange zest
150 g (5½ oz/1 cup) plain (all-purpose) flour
1 teaspoon baking powder
¼ teaspoon salt
butter, for cooking
Greek-style yoghurt, to serve

ORANGE SYRUP
375 ml (13 fl oz/1½ cups) fresh orange juice (about 3 oranges)
2 oranges, peeled, white pith removed and roughly chopped
1 tablespoon caster (superfine) sugar

To make the orange syrup, place all of the ingredients into a small saucepan and bring to the boil. Reduce the heat to low and simmer for 20 minutes, or until the sauce thickens. You will need to reheat the syrup briefly before serving.

In a large bowl, whisk together the egg yolks and sugar until creamy. Add the ricotta, milk and orange zest and beat until smooth. In a separate bowl, sift together the flour, baking powder and salt. Fold into the ricotta mixture and stir until well combined.

Heat a little butter in a large frying pan over medium–low heat. Add ⅓ cup of the batter to the pan at a time, smoothing the mixture out with a spoon so each hotcake makes a neat circle. Cook for a few minutes, until bubbles form and the hotcake is just about cooked through, then flip and fry for a further minute on the other side. As they cook, transfer the hotcakes to a plate lined with paper towel. Repeat with the remaining mixture until all cooked — you should make about 10 hotcakes in total.

Serve the hotcakes drizzled with the warm orange syrup and a generous dollop of Greek-style yoghurt.

Artwork by
Rachael Bartram
mixed media on paper

Invitation

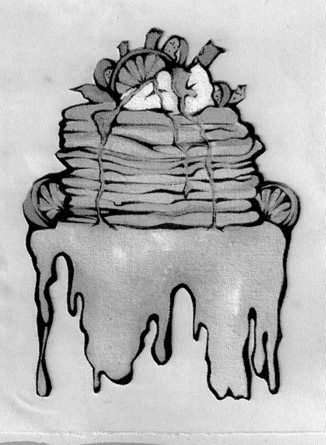

Dips and pieces

There is something special about a platter of different tastes —
a cheese and cracker here, an olive there, the swirl of a dip, the
nibble of a tart. This chapter provides a mix and match of
biscuits, dips and small bites, whether its for that well-earned
Friday afternoon platter, party bits, a picnic spread, or for a
quiet moment with a plate to yourself.

Fig salami

Don't judge this fruity log by its appearance — it has a musty, nostalgic taste, as if it should be enjoyed in the company of great philosophers, poets and artists. Full of zest and the rich flavours of orange, cinnamon and brandy, slices of this 'salami' are the perfect accompaniment to cheese.

PREPARATION TIME: 20 MINUTES + 2 DAYS REFRIGERATION
COOKING TIME: NIL
SERVES: 10+

200 g (7 oz) dried figs
200 g (7 oz) pitted dates
125 g (4½ oz/1 cup) roughly chopped walnuts
½ teaspoon ground cinnamon
1 tablespoon brandy
2 teaspoons finely grated lemon zest
2 teaspoons finely grated orange zest
1 teaspoon natural vanilla extract or scrape
    the seeds from ½ vanilla bean

Put the figs and dates in a blender or food processor and blend or process until finely chopped. Transfer to a large bowl and combine with all of the remaining ingredients, mixing well. Turn the mixture out onto a clean work surface and divide into two equal portions. Shape each portion into a 20 cm (8 inch) log, pressing firmly together.

Wrap each log separately in baking paper and twist the ends to seal, then tie up using kitchen string. Allow to set in the refrigerator for 2 days before serving.

Artwork by
Luke Brown
digital collage

Platter trappings

To really impress your guests, embellish your cheese platter with a selection of these tasty assortments.

PREPARATION TIME: 20 MINUTES
COOKING TIME: 30 MINUTES
SERVES: 10+

Whole roasted garlic cloves

2 whole garlic bulbs
1 tablespoon olive oil

Preheat the oven to 180°C (350°F/Gas 4). Slice just enough off the top of each garlic bulb to reveal the cloves. Place on a baking tray and drizzle with the olive oil. Bake in the oven for 30 minutes, or until soft. Serve warm.

Watermelon and prosciutto bites

50 g (1¾ oz) prosciutto, torn in strips lengthways
¼ watermelon, cut into 2 cm (¾ inch) wedges
5 g (⅛ oz/¼ cup) basil, torn
olive oil, to drizzle

Wrap strips of prosciutto around the watermelon wedges, with a little basil in each parcel. Drizzle with olive oil and sprinkle with freshly ground black pepper.

Warm olives

2 tablespoons olive oil
200 g (7 oz) mixed unflavoured whole olives
1 teaspoon thyme
1 teaspoon finely grated orange zest

Heat the olive oil in a saucepan over medium heat. Add the olives, thyme and orange zest and cook for about 5 minutes, tossing constantly to prevent the olives from burning. Remove from the heat and serve immediately.

Artwork by
Emico Isobe
acrylic on wood

Dolmades

There's something undeniably soothing about making these traditional Greek vine-leaf parcels — the way your mind wanders when rolling them, occasionally munching on the salty leaves to get a taste of what's to come. These are cooked in a tomato passata, making them extra juicy, and it also helps break through the acidity of the pickled vine leaves.

PREPARATION TIME: 30 MINUTES
COOKING TIME: 1 HOUR 5 MINUTES
MAKES: ABOUT 50

200 ml (7 fl oz) olive oil
1 onion, diced
200 g (7 oz/1 cup) long-grain rice
100 g (3½ oz/⅔ cup) pine nuts
25 g (1 oz/¾ cup) finely chopped
  flat-leaf (Italian) parsley

15 g (½ oz/¼ cup) finely
  chopped dill
250 g (9 oz) packet vine leaves
500–750 ml (17–26 fl oz/2–3 cups)
  tomato passata (puréed
  tomatoes)

Preheat the oven to 180°C (350°F/Gas 4). Heat the olive oil in a large saucepan over medium–low heat. Add the onion and cook gently until soft, about 8 minutes. Add the rice and stir for a couple of minutes, then add 375 ml (13 fl oz/1½ cups) water, the pine nuts, parsley and dill. Cook, uncovered, for 15 minutes — all of the liquid should be absorbed. Remove from the heat and season with sea salt and freshly ground black pepper, to taste.

Separate the vine leaves and lightly rinse them to remove any brine. Lay the vine leaves, vein side up — the smooth side should be on the outside of the rolled dolmades. Place a tablespoon of the rice mixture at one end of a leaf and roll up tightly, folding in the sides to make a neat cigar shape. Repeat until all of the rice mixture is used.

Arrange any broken or leftover leaves in the base of a 20 x 30 cm (8 x 12 inch) baking dish. Place the dolmades in rows, stacking them in two neat layers. Arrange a few remaining vine leaves on top, then pour over enough of the tomato passata to fill the dish almost to the top layer of the dolmades.

Bake the dolmades in the oven for 35–40 minutes, or until the passata has been absorbed. Remove from the oven and allow to cool completely. Dolmades are best served cold or at room temperature. They keep for about 1 week in the refrigerator, but they never last longer than a day in our house.

Artwork by
Naomi Lees–Maiberg
watercolour on paper

Dip selection

PREPARATION TIME: 15 MINUTES PER DIP
COOKING TIME: 40 MINUTES FOR ROASTED EGGPLANT DIP

Black olive tapenade

MAKES: 1⅓ CUPS

225 g (8 oz/1½ cups) pitted black kalamata olives
55 g (2 oz/⅓ cup) sun-dried or semi-dried (sun-blushed) tomatoes
1 tablespoon capers, rinsed and squeezed dry
2 anchovy fillets, roughly chopped
60 ml (2 fl oz/¼ cup) olive oil, plus extra for drizzling

Put all of the ingredients into a food processor and blend until a paste forms. Season with a little sea salt, to taste, then transfer to a serving bowl.

Artichoke and white bean dip

MAKES: 2 CUPS

340 g (11¾ oz) tinned artichoke hearts, drained and liquid reserved
400 g (14 oz) tin cannellini or butter beans (lima beans), rinsed and drained
1 tablespoon olive oil, plus extra for drizzling

Put the artichoke hearts in a food processor with the beans and olive oil and process until just smooth, adding a little of the reserved artichoke liquid if needed; season to taste. Transfer to a serving bowl and drizzle with extra olive oil.

Roasted eggplant dip

MAKES: 1⅓ CUPS

1 large eggplant (aubergine)
1 tablespoon finely chopped flat-leaf (Italian) parsley
1 teaspoon red wine vinegar
½ garlic clove, finely chopped
1 tablespoon olive oil, plus extra for drizzling

Preheat the oven to 200°C (400°F/Gas 6). Prick the eggplant with a fork in several places and place on a baking tray. Roast in the oven for 35–40 minutes, or until the eggplant is soft. Set aside to cool for 10 minutes.

Roughly chop the eggplant and place in a food processor with the remaining ingredients and blend until smooth. If making by hand, halve the eggplant and scoop out the flesh then mash together with the remaining ingredients. Season with sea salt and freshly ground black pepper, then transfer to a serving bowl and drizzle with extra olive oil to serve.

Artwork by
Joe Baker
digital illustration

Lovely legs

Everyone appreciates a nice set of legs! Administer these tangy, medieval-like snacks with moist towelettes as they are super sticky.

PREPARATION TIME: 15 MINUTES + 1 HOUR REFRIGERATION
COOKING TIME: 40 MINUTES
SERVES: 8

80 ml (2½ fl oz/⅓ cup) soy sauce
2 tablespoons caster (superfine) sugar
1 tablespoon fish sauce
2 teaspoons lime juice
2 teaspoons finely grated ginger
¼ teaspoon chilli powder
2 tablespoons grapeseed oil
2 tablespoons finely chopped coriander
   (cilantro) leaves and stems
8 chicken drumsticks

In a bowl, combine the soy sauce, sugar, fish sauce, lime juice, ginger and chilli, and stir until the sugar has dissolved. Add the grapeseed oil and coriander and mix well.

Arrange the chicken drumsticks in a 20 cm (8 inch) square baking dish, pour over the marinade and toss well to coat. Cover and refrigerate for at least 1 hour, or preferably overnight, turning the drumsticks occasionally.

Preheat the oven to 180°C (350°F/Gas 4). Roast the drumsticks in the oven for 20 minutes, then turn them over to coat in the juices and roast for a further 15–20 minutes, or until cooked through. Remove from the oven and serve hot.

Artwork by
Inés Iglesias
watercolour on paper

Japanese rice slice

These pretty little squares of layered rice and smoked salmon are decorated with sesame seeds, but you can also use bonito flakes, nori and roe. The delicate flavours make them versatile for party platters, packed lunches or even breakfast.

PREPARATION TIME: 30 MINUTES + REFRIGERATION
COOKING TIME: 20 MINUTES
SERVES: 10+

2 tablespoons rice vinegar
1 tablespoon caster (superfine) sugar
½ teaspoon salt
350 g (12 oz/1⅔ cups) sushi rice
2 tablespoons Japanese mayonnaise
200 g (7 oz) smoked salmon slices
75 g (2¾ oz/½ cup) black or white sesame seeds
soy sauce, to serve

In a bowl, combine the rice vinegar, sugar and salt and stir well until the sugar has dissolved.

Put 700 ml (24 fl oz) water in a saucepan and bring to the boil. Add the rice, stir well and bring back to the boil. Reduce the heat to low, cover tightly with a lid, and simmer for 15 minutes. Remove the pan from the heat, stir through the vinegar seasoning and use a fork to stir and fluff up the rice grains.

Line a 28 x 30 cm (11¼ x 12 inch) baking tin with plastic wrap extending over the two long sides. Press the rice firmly into the tin, cover with the plastic wrap and refrigerate until needed.

Lift the rice from the tin using the overhanging plastic as handles. Cut the rice slab in half through the centre. Spread both halves of the rice with a thin layer of mayonnaise, then top with the salmon. Fold one side of rice over the other to make a sandwich. Use a sharp knife dipped in hot water to cut into small squares. Place the sesame seeds on a large plate and dip the top of each rice square into the seeds to coat. Serve with soy sauce.

Artwork by
Jack Douglas
pen on paper

समोसा सुभोसा चिऽऊद्ध
ಸಮೋಸಾ சமோசா

Samosas with chutneys

Samosas are one of those foods that rarely get turned down. They are the ultimate crowd-pleasing party snack. If you're not up for making the pastry you can use ready-made puff or spring roll pastry instead.

PREPARATION TIME: 1 HOUR + 30 MINUTES RESTING
COOKING TIME: 1 HOUR
MAKES: ABOUT 20

SAMOSA PASTRY
225 g (8 oz/1½ cups) plain (all-purpose) flour
3 tablespoons semolina
½ teaspoon salt
60 ml (2 fl oz/¼ cup) grapeseed oil

SAMOSA FILLING
1 tablespoon grapeseed oil
1 small onion, halved and thinly sliced
½ teaspoon cumin seeds
40 g (1½ oz/¼ cup) cashews, roughly chopped
180 g (6½ oz) all-purpose potatoes, peeled, boiled and roughly mashed
½ long green chilli, seeded and finely chopped
7 g (¼ oz/¼ cup) coriander (cilantro) leaves and stems, chopped
35 g (1¼ oz/¼ cup) baby green peas
½ teaspoon garam masala
2 tablespoons currants
1 tablespoon lemon juice
½ teaspoon salt

TOMATO CHUTNEY
80 ml (2½ fl oz/⅓ cup) grapeseed oil
1 red onion, thinly sliced into rings
1 tablespoon ground turmeric
1 tablespoon brown mustard seeds
2 teaspoons ground cumin
400 g (14 oz) tin whole tomatoes, chopped
60 ml (2 fl oz/¼ cup) cider vinegar
45 g (1¾ oz/¼ cup) soft brown sugar

YOGHURT TAMARIND CHUTNEY
½ teaspoon ground cumin seeds
260 g (9¼ oz/1 cup) plain yoghurt
2 tablespoons tamarind paste
½ teaspoon chilli powder

To make the samosa pastry, mix together the flour, semolina and salt in a bowl. Combine the grapeseed oil and 80 ml (2½ fl oz/⅓ cup) warm water, then add to the dry ingredients, using your hands to bring the dough together, adding a little more water if necessary. Once the dough comes together easily, turn out onto a lightly floured work surface and knead for 5 minutes until smooth. Wrap the pastry in plastic wrap and set aside to rest for 30 minutes.

Artwork by
Kai Noland
mixed media on watercolour paper

CONTINUED ➜

To make the samosa filling, heat the grapeseed oil in a saucepan over medium–high heat. Add the onion and cook for 2–3 minutes, or until golden. Reduce the heat to medium, add the cumin seeds and cashews and cook for a further 2 minutes. Add the potato and 2 tablespoons water and continue to cook, stirring for a further 2–3 minutes. Remove from the heat, add the remaining filling ingredients and stir well to combine. Set aside to cool.

To assemble the samosas, divide the pastry into ten even-sized portions. Roll each portion into a 15 cm (6 inch) circle. Cut each circle in half to make semi-circles. Arrange each semi-circle with the straight edge at the top. Fold the sides in towards the centre so they slightly overlap and press to seal, keeping them separate from the back, to create a 'pocket'. Press a couple of teaspoons of mixture inside each samosa pocket. Seal the open end by folding over the pastry and pressing the sides firmly together, then curl over the edges. Repeat with the remaining pastry and filling and set aside.

To cook the samosas, fill a large heavy-based saucepan with enough oil so that it is about 4 cm (1½ inches) deep and heat the oil — it is hot enough when a little pastry is dropped into the oil and it bubbles furiously. Lower the samosas into the hot oil, in batches, and deep-fry for 2–3 minutes, or until golden brown — it is best to start cooking the samosas over low heat and gradually increase the heat, which will make the pastry crisp. Drain on paper towel and serve hot with the tomato and yoghurt tamarind chutneys.

To make the tomato chutney, heat the oil in a saucepan over medium–low heat. Add the onion and cook for about 5 minutes, or until it has softened. Add the turmeric, mustard seeds and cumin and cook for 2 minutes, or until the mustard seeds start to pop. Add the tomatoes, vinegar and sugar and simmer, stirring often, over medium–low heat for 20–30 minutes, or until the chutney is thick and rich. Season with sea salt and refrigerate until ready to serve.

To make the yoghurt tamarind chutney, dry-fry the cumin seeds in a small frying pan for about 20 seconds over medium heat, or until fragrant. Remove from the heat and add to a bowl with the remaining ingredients, stirring well to combine. Refrigerate until ready to serve. Both chutneys can be stored in the refrigerator for up to 4 days.

Trio of tarts

A quintessential picnic or party feature, tarts are easy to make and can have enormous variation in toppings. You can use homemade or ready-made puff, filo or shortcrust pastry (page 83) for these tarts.

PREPARATION TIME: 30 MINUTES
COOKING TIME: 30 MINUTES FOR TARTS
  + 35 MINUTES EXTRA FOR ONION JAM
SERVES: EACH TART SERVES 6 AS A STARTER

Tomato and thyme tart

170 g (6 oz/1 sheet) puff pastry
350 g (12 oz/2 cups) cherry
  tomatoes, halved
3 garlic cloves, finely chopped
1 tablespoon thyme, finely chopped

1½ tablespoons olive oil
1½ tablespoons dijon mustard
1 egg yolk mixed with
  2 tablespoons water

Preheat the oven to 180°C (350°F/Gas 4). Line a baking tray with baking paper. Roll out or trim the pastry to make a 20 x 30 cm (8 x 12 inch) rectangle, about 2.5 mm (1/16 inch) thick. Place the pastry on the prepared tray.

Combine the tomatoes, garlic, thyme and olive oil in a bowl and season with sea salt and freshly ground black pepper. Spread the pastry with mustard, leaving a 2 cm (¾ inch) border around the edges. Arrange the tomatoes, cut side up, over the pastry — this will avoid making the tart soggy. Fold over the pastry edges that have been left as a border and brush with the eggwash.

Bake the tart in the oven for about 30 minutes, or until the tomatoes are soft and the pastry is golden. Remove from the oven, cut into slices and serve hot.

Pissaladiere

170 g (6 oz/1 sheet) puff pastry
10 anchovy fillets
95 g (3¼ oz/½ cup) pitted and
  chopped kalamata olives
1 egg yolk mixed with
  2 tablespoons water

ONION JAM
125 ml (4 fl oz/½ cup) olive oil
1 kg (2 lb 4 oz) brown onions, thinly
  sliced into rings
1 bay leaf
1 tablespoon soft brown sugar
1 tablespoon balsamic vinegar
  or red wine vinegar
a pinch of salt

Preheat the oven to 180°C (350°F/Gas 4). Line a baking tray with baking paper. Roll out or trim the pastry to make a 20 x 30 cm (8 x 12 inch) rectangle, about 2.5 mm (1/16 inch) thick. Place the pastry on the prepared tray.

To make the onion jam, heat the olive oil in a large saucepan over medium heat. Add the onion, bay leaf, sugar, vinegar and salt and stir for 3–4 minutes, or until the sugar has dissolved. Reduce the heat to low and cook for about 30 minutes, stirring occasionally to avoid the onion sticking to the pan and burning — it should be thick and jammy. Remove from the heat and allow to cool.

Spread the onion jam over the tart base leaving a 2 cm (¾ inch) border around the edges. Top with the anchovies, olives and freshly ground black pepper. Fold over the pastry edges that have been left as a border and brush with the eggwash. Bake the tart in the oven for 20–30 minutes, or until the pastry is golden. Remove from the oven, cut into slices and serve hot.

Shaved zucchini, mint and feta tart

170 g (6 oz/1 sheet) puff pastry
2 zucchini (courgettes), shaved thinly using a potato peeler
150 g (5½ oz) feta cheese, crumbled
1 teaspoon finely grated lemon zest
2 tablespoons olive oil
25 g (1 oz/½ cup) finely chopped mint
1 egg yolk mixed with 2 tablespoons water

Preheat the oven to 180°C (350°F/Gas 4). Line a baking tray with baking paper. Roll out or trim the pastry to make a 20 x 30 cm (8 x 12 inch) rectangle, about 2.5 mm (1/16 inch) thick. Place the pastry on the prepared tray.

In a bowl, combine the zucchini, feta, lemon zest and olive oil. Season well and toss to mix thoroughly. Spread the mixture evenly over the tart base, leaving a 2 cm (¾ inch) border around the edges. Fold over the pastry edges that have been left as a border and brush with the eggwash.

Bake the tart in the oven for 20–30 minutes, or until the pastry is golden. Remove from the oven, scatter over the mint, cut into slices and serve hot.

Artwork by
Archie Lee Coates
illustration

Soups

Soups allow for endless creativity and experimentation in the kitchen, and are a great way to use up what's left in your vegetable drawer. The soups in this chapter can work as appetisers or light meals — diverse in cuisine and flavour, they are 'souped up' with a little something extra, from a herby drizzle to parmesan toasts.

Onion and Champagne soup with parmesan toasts

This soup started life as onion and apple cider soup, but having no cider one day, and a glass of Champagne at hand, we substituted the cider for Champagne and have never looked back!

PREPARATION TIME: 15 MINUTES
COOKING TIME: 1 HOUR
SERVES: 4

40 g (1½ oz) butter
1 kg (2 lb 4 oz) brown onions, thinly sliced into rings
1 bay leaf
250 ml (9 fl oz/1 cup) Champagne or sparkling white wine
500 ml (17 fl oz/2 cups) beef stock

PARMESAN TOASTS
8 slices sourdough bread
dijon mustard (optional)
100 g (3½ oz/¾ cup) finely grated parmesan cheese

To make the soup, melt the butter in a large saucepan over medium heat. Add the onion and bay leaf, cover and cook for 30 minutes, or until the onion has started to caramelise. Stir regularly to remove any onion sticking to the base of the pan.

Remove the lid from the pan, add the Champagne and cook the soup for a further 10 minutes over medium–low heat. Add the stock and 250 ml (9 fl oz/1 cup) water, bring to the boil, then reduce the heat to low and simmer, uncovered, for a further 15 minutes, or until the soup thickens.

To make the parmesan toasts, preheat the griller (broiler) to high. Spread the mustard, if using, over the sourdough slices, and then top with the grated parmesan. Place under the griller until the cheese is melted and golden.

Divide the soup between serving bowls and serve with the parmesan toasts and remaining Champagne.

Artwork by
Inés Iglesias
watercolour on paper

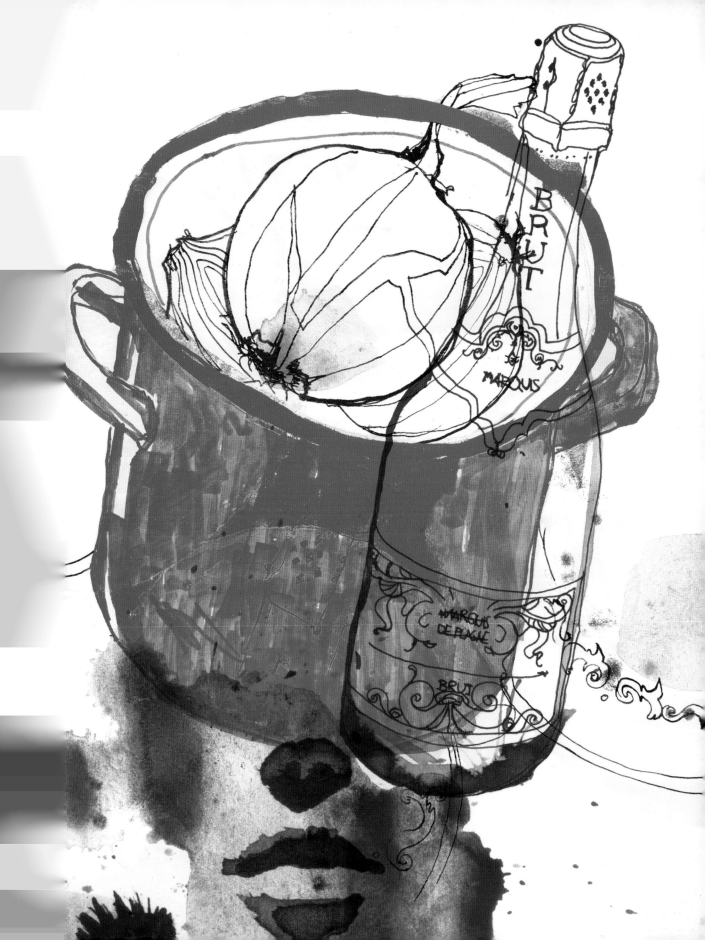

Thai pumpkin soup with coriander drizzle

Deviating from the traditional 'ye olde' pumpkin soup flavour profile of cream and nutmeg, this pumpkin soup is a fresh, vibrant version with an Asian influence. The tangy citrus drizzle, thinly sliced red onions and chilli provide extra zing.

PREPARATION TIME: 20 MINUTES
COOKING TIME: 45 MINUTES
SERVES: 4

2 tablespoons olive oil
1 onion, finely chopped
1 heaped tablespoon finely grated
    ginger
3 tablespoons red curry paste
1.2 kg (2 lb 10 oz) pumpkin (winter
    squash), peeled, seeded and
    roughly chopped
750 ml (26 fl oz/3 cups) vegetable
    or chicken stock
250 ml (9 fl oz/1 cup) coconut milk

plain yoghurt or sour cream,
    to serve
½ red onion, finely chopped,
    to serve
1 bird's eye red chilli, seeded
    and thinly sliced, to serve

CORIANDER DRIZZLE
2 tablespoons olive oil
100 ml (3½ fl oz) lemon juice
25 g (1 oz/½ cup) finely chopped
    coriander (cilantro) leaves

To make the soup, heat the olive oil in a large saucepan over medium–low heat. Add the onion and ginger and cook for 4–5 minutes, or until the onion is translucent. Add the red curry paste and cook for a further few minutes, or until fragrant. Stir in the pumpkin, add the stock, bring to the boil, then reduce the heat to low and simmer gently for about 20 minutes, or until the pumpkin is soft.

Transfer the pumpkin and stock to a blender or food processor and blend or process until smooth. Return the soup to a clean saucepan over medium–low heat and stir in the coconut milk. Continue to simmer for a further 10 minutes.

To make the coriander drizzle, put the olive oil, lemon juice and coriander in a bowl and stir well to combine.

To serve, divide the soup between bowls topped with a little coriander drizzle, then garnish with the yoghurt, onion and chilli.

Artwork by
Warren Handley
digital illustration

Asian moules frites

This soup puts an Asian spin on a European classic. Characteristic Belgian flavours of parsley and cream are substituted with Asian favourites coriander and fish sauce. You can leave your utensils in the drawer when serving — use the empty mussel shells to slurp up the soup, and the frites to soak up the juices.

PREPARATION TIME: 30 MINUTES + 20 MINUTES INFUSING
COOKING TIME: 1 HOUR 10 MINUTES
SERVES: 4

MOULES
½ teaspoon saffron threads
125 ml (4 fl oz/½ cup) dry
    white wine
125 ml (4 fl oz/½ cup) fish or
    chicken stock
2 makrut (kaffir lime) leaves,
    very thinly sliced
1 teaspoon fish sauce
1 tablespoon finely grated ginger
1 garlic clove, finely chopped
1 long red chilli, seeded and
    finely chopped
10 g (¼ oz/⅓ cup) coriander
    (cilantro) stems, roughly
    chopped
1 kg (2 lb 4 oz) mussels, debearded
    and washed
15 g (½ oz/½ cup) coriander
    (cilantro) leaves
1 tablespoon lime juice
lime wedges, to serve

FRITES
1 kg (2 lb 4 oz/about 3 large)
    floury potatoes, such as sebago
60 ml (2 fl oz/¼ cup) olive oil

To make the *frites*, preheat the oven to 200°C (400°F/Gas 6). Wash the potatoes and slice into thick chips. Dry thoroughly with paper towel. Place the dried chips on a baking tray, drizzle with the olive oil, season with sea salt and freshly ground black pepper and toss to coat. Bake the chips for about 1 hour, turning occasionally, until crisp and golden.

To make the *moules*, combine the saffron threads and white wine in a bowl and set aside for 20 minutes to infuse. Combine the stock and kaffir leaves in a large saucepan and bring to the boil. Reduce the heat to medium and simmer for 1 minute, then add the white wine and saffron mixture, fish sauce, ginger, garlic, chilli and coriander stems. Stir well and simmer for a further minute.

Increase the heat to medium–high, add the mussels to the pan and toss well to combine, then cover and cook for 2–3 minutes, or until the mussels start to open. Gently toss through the coriander leaves and lime juice and cook for a further minute or two, or until all of the mussels open. Discard any unopened mussels.

Divide the mussels and broth between serving bowls and serve with the *frites* and lime wedges on the side.

Artwork by
Max Berry
acrylic on paper

HOW TO FOLD A WONTON

Samosa Style

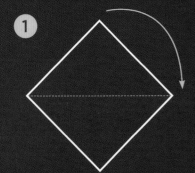

1 Rotate your wonton wrapper 45°.

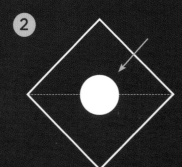

2 Place your filling in the centre.

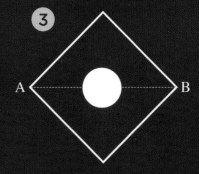

3 Gently pinch sides 'A' and 'B' between fingertips.

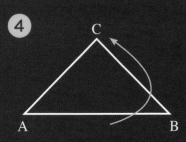

4 Add water to the corners, fold the wrapper in half. Push out air between the wrapper and filling.

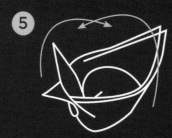

5 Wet the two side corners of the triangle, pull them together, press firmly. The centre corner should stick out slightly.

6 Boil the wonton in water. **Serve and enjoy!**

The number of ways to fold wontons is limited only by imagination

Prawn wonton broth

This broth tastes deeply cleansing and nourishing. Making the wontons will leave you with a sense of accomplishment and is a transferable skill — you'll be able to craft all sorts of parcels, such as spinach and ricotta ravioli, mushroom tortellini or pork gyoza. Pop them in a soup, serve them with a sauce, steam or fry them.

PREPARATION TIME: 1 HOUR
COOKING TIME: 35 MINUTES
SERVES: 4 (MAKES ABOUT 20 WONTONS)

PRAWN WONTONS

- 500 g (1 lb 2 oz) raw prawns (shrimp), peeled and deveined
- 1 tablespoon finely grated ginger
- 3 spring onions (scallions), finely chopped
- 1 tablespoon chopped coriander (cilantro) leaves
- 2 teaspoons sesame seeds
- 1 teaspoon sesame oil
- ½ egg, lightly beaten
- ½ teaspoon white pepper
- ½ teaspoon salt
- 20 wonton wrappers

BROTH

- 80 ml (2½ fl oz/⅓ cup) grapeseed oil
- 1 teaspoon sesame oil
- 1 red onion, roughly chopped
- 6 garlic cloves, sliced
- 1 tablespoon finely grated ginger
- 2 lemongrass stems, bruised and cut into 2.5 cm (1 inch) pieces
- 6 makrut (kaffir lime) leaves
- 50 g (1¾ oz/1 cup) roughly chopped coriander (cilantro) leaves and stems, plus extra leaves to serve
- 2 bird's eye chillies, seeded and chopped
- 500 ml (17 fl oz/2 cups) chicken stock
- 80 ml (2½ fl oz/⅓ cup) fish sauce
- 1 tablespoon grated palm sugar (jaggery) or soft brown sugar
- 80 ml (2½ fl oz/⅓ cup) lime juice
- Asian greens, to serve (optional)
- lime wedges, to serve

To make the wontons, finely chop the prawns and add to a bowl with the ginger, spring onion, coriander, sesame seeds, sesame oil, egg, white pepper and salt and mix well to combine.

Place a teaspoon of the mixture into the centre of each wonton wrapper. Fold each wrapper in half and press the edges together, sealing with a little water. You can fold the wrappers again, depending on the aesthetic you like. Alternatively, you can pull all the sides up together to create a 'money bag' shape. Place on a floured tray and refrigerate until needed.

Artwork by
Adel Cox
digital illustration

CONTINUED ➜➜

To make the broth, heat the grapeseed and sesame oil in a large saucepan over medium heat. Add the onion, garlic and ginger and cook until the onion has softened. Add the lemongrass, kaffir lime leaves, coriander and chilli. Cook for a couple of minutes, then add the stock and 2.5 litres (87 fl oz/10 cups) water and bring just to the boil. Reduce the heat to low and simmer for 20 minutes. Remove from the heat and strain, reserving the stock and discarding the flavourings.

Return the stock to the saucepan, stir in the fish sauce, palm sugar and lime juice, and season with salt, to taste. Bring to the boil, then add the wontons — when they rise to the surface, cook for 2 minutes longer. You can add Asian greens, such as bok choy (pak choy) at this stage. Serve the soup sprinkled with coriander leaves and lime wedges on the side.

Roasted tomato and zucchini soup with olive bread

Roasting the vegetables in this Mediterranean soup provides a deeper, richer flavour. Enjoy this soup hot or cold with the olive-dotted bread.

PREPARATION TIME: 45 MINUTES + 1 HOUR DOUGH PROVING
 + 30 MINUTES RISING FOR BREAD
COOKING TIME: 1 HOUR 15 MINUTES
SERVES: 4

1 kg (2 lb 4 oz/about 8–10) tomatoes, halved
700 g (1 lb 9 oz/about 4–5) large zucchini (courgettes), halved lengthways
2 onions, quartered
1 whole garlic bulb, with the top cut off
olive oil, for drizzling
shaved parmesan cheese, to serve

OLIVE BREAD
7 g (¼ oz/2 teaspoons) active dried yeast
450 g (1 lb/3 cups) plain (all-purpose) flour
1 tablespoon caster (superfine) sugar
1 teaspoon salt
2 tablespoons olive oil
30 g (1 oz/½ cup) roughly chopped basil
150 g (5½ oz/1 cup) pitted kalamata olives, roughly chopped

To make the olive bread, whisk together the yeast and 310 ml (10¾ fl oz/1¼ cups) warm water in a small bowl. Allow to stand for about 10 minutes, or until the mixture starts to froth. Combine the flour, sugar and salt in a large mixing bowl and stir to combine. Make a well in the centre then add the yeast mixture and olive oil and mix together. Turn the dough out onto a lightly floured work surface and knead for 10 minutes, or until the dough is smooth and elastic. Place in an oiled bowl, cover with a clean damp tea towel (dish towel) and set aside for about 1 hour, or until the dough has doubled in size.

Heat the oven to 220°C (425°F/Gas 7). Lightly grease a baking tray. Punch down the dough and knead again for about 5 minutes. Spread the dough out, scatter over the basil and olives and knead to evenly distribute them through the dough, then shape into a round. Place onto the prepared tray and allow to rise for about 30 minutes. Bake the bread in the oven for 30 minutes, or until it is golden and sounds hollow when tapped on the base.

CONTINUED →→

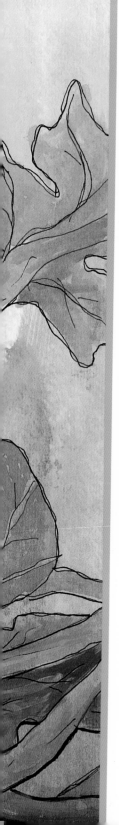

To make the roasted tomato and zucchini soup, preheat the oven to 180°C (350°F/Gas 4). Place the tomatoes, zucchini, onion and garlic in a large roasting dish. Drizzle with olive oil, season with sea salt and freshly ground black pepper and toss to coat. Roast the vegetables in the oven for 30 minutes, or until soft.

Remove the vegetables from the oven and allow to cool slightly. Squeeze the roasted garlic into a blender or food processor, discarding the skins, and scrape in all the other vegetables. Add 500 ml (17 fl oz/2 cups) hot water and blend until smooth.

Transfer the soup to a large saucepan over medium–high heat and bring to the boil. Reduce the heat to low and simmer for 15 minutes. Check the seasoning and serve the soup with shaved parmesan and buttered slices of the olive bread.

Artwork by
Helen Schroeder
watercolour on paper

Mexican bean soup

Simple, cheap and comforting, this soup is perfect for mid-week dining and feeding a crowd. You can serve it with a lively assortment of toppings — make it heartier with some fried chorizo, healthier with chunks of avocado, creamier with a dollop of sour cream or spicier with some chilli.

PREPARATION TIME: 20 MINUTES
COOKING TIME: 25 MINUTES
SERVES: 4

2 x 400 g (14 oz) tins kidney beans,
    rinsed and drained
2 small brown onions, roughly chopped
2 tablespoons olive oil
2 x 400 g (14 oz) tins whole tomatoes,
    roughly chopped
100 g (3½ oz) cheddar cheese,
    cut into 1 cm (½ inch) cubes

TO SERVE
1 chorizo, sliced and fried
1 avocado, cut into chunks
plain yoghurt or sour cream
freshly chopped chilli or sambal oelek
corn chips or toasted pitta bread

Combine the kidney beans and onion in a food processor and process to make a rough paste.

Heat the olive oil in a large saucepan over medium heat, add the bean mixture and cook for about 1 minute. Add the tomatoes and 125 ml (4 fl oz/½ cup) water, bring to the boil, then reduce the heat to low and simmer for about 20 minutes. Season to taste with sea salt and freshly ground black pepper — you may need to add more water if you like a thinner soup.

To serve, divide the cubes of cheese between serving bowls and pour over the hot soup. Garnish with your preferred toppings and serve immediately.

Artwork by
RYOONO
digital illustration

Pean ham soup

For most of her formative years, Georgie thought there was a special type of vegetable called a 'pean', used especially for pea and ham soup. This soup is a winter favourite — hearty and warming — and it gets better with age. The family dog will love you for the leftover bacon bones.

PREPARATION TIME: 20 MINUTES + 8 HOURS SOAKING
COOKING TIME: 2 HOURS 20 MINUTES
SERVES: 4–6

500 g (1 lb 2 oz/2¼ cups) dried green or yellow split peas
40 g (1½ oz) butter
2 onions, roughly chopped
2 garlic cloves, finely chopped
4 celery stalks, finely chopped
2 carrots, finely chopped
1 kg (2 lb 4 oz) ham hock (you can use smoked or raw, or use bacon bones if unavailable)
2 bay leaves

Place the dried peas in a large bowl, pour in enough water to cover the peas by 5 cm (2 inches), and set aside to soak for 8 hours or overnight. Rinse the peas, drain well and set aside.

In a large saucepan, melt the butter over medium–low heat. Add the onion, garlic, celery and carrot, cover, and cook for 8–10 minutes, stirring occasionally, until the onion is translucent. Increase the heat to medium, add the ham hock and cook for a few minutes until it begins to brown.

Add the bay leaves to the pan with just enough water to cover the hock. Bring to the boil, then reduce the heat to low, cover, and simmer for 1 hour. Add the peas and a little more water to cover all the ingredients, season with sea salt and freshly ground black pepper, and continue to simmer, stirring occasionally, until the peas are tender, about 1 hour.

Remove the pan from the heat and remove the ham hock from the soup. When cool enough to handle, remove the meat from the bone, discarding the skin and fat and shredding the meat. Blend the soup until smooth, then return the shredded meat to the soup. Reheat to serve, adding more water if the soup becomes too thick or dry.

Artwork by
Erin Smith and Jo Pole
digital illustration

Mains

In this chapter you'll find some simple dishes for midweek dining, and some that require more time and attention — all are designed to excite the senses, stimulate conversation and provide a treasured moment to reflect, as well as something delicious to eat! These meals have a wide variety of flavours and use ingredients from different cuisines, from semolina gnocchi to tandoori salmon and star anise-spiced prawns to lamb and prune tagine.

Eggplant mozzarella bake

This dish is the ultimate comfort food — warm and satisfying, with bubbling cheese and meaty eggplant. Salting the eggplant is not absolutely necessary but it helps to draw out any bitterness and also decreases the amount of oil the eggplant will absorb.

PREPARATION TIME: 30 MINUTES + 30 MINUTES SALTING FOR THE EGGPLANT
COOKING TIME: 1 HOUR 40 MINUTES
SERVES: 4

80 ml (2½ fl oz/⅓ cup) olive oil
2 large or 3 medium eggplants (aubergines), sliced into 1 cm (½ inch) rounds
20 g (¾ oz) butter
1 brown onion, finely chopped
4 garlic cloves, finely chopped
2 x 400 g (14 oz) tins whole tomatoes, roughly chopped
1 teaspoon caster (superfine) sugar
1 teaspoon salt, plus extra for salting eggplant
1 tablespoon finely chopped oregano or marjoram
250 g (9 oz) mozzarella cheese, thinly sliced
100 g (3½ oz/¾ cup) finely grated parmesan cheese

Preheat the oven to 180°C (350°F/Gas 4). Grease a 30 cm (12 inch) square baking dish with a little olive oil.

Place the eggplant in a colander. Sprinkle some salt over the eggplant and toss well. Set aside for 30–60 minutes for the moisture to be drawn out. Rinse well and pat dry with paper towel, making sure the eggplant pieces have been dried well.

Heat the butter in a saucepan over medium–low heat. Add the onion and garlic and cook until soft and translucent, about 5–8 minutes. Stir in the tomatoes, sugar and salt and season with freshly ground black pepper. Increase the heat and bring to the boil, then reduce the heat to low and simmer gently for about 30 minutes, stirring occasionally. Remove from the heat, stir in the oregano or marjoram and taste for seasoning.

Heat a little olive oil in a large frying pan over medium–high heat. Add the eggplant, in batches, and cook for 1–2 minutes on each side, or until lightly browned, then drain on paper towel. Repeat until all of the eggplant is cooked, adding a little extra oil as needed, but avoid adding too much or the dish will become greasy.

Place a layer of eggplant slices in the baking dish, top with half of the tomato sauce, then a layer of mozzarella. Repeat with another layer of eggplant, tomato sauce and mozzarella. Sprinkle the last layer of mozzarella with the parmesan cheese. Bake in the oven for about 30 minutes, or until the cheese is bubbling and golden brown. Cut into slices and serve.

Artwork by
Katie Willmett
pencil on paper

BEETROOT WALNUT RISOTTO GOATSCHEESE

Beetroot, goat's cheese and walnut risotto

When you add the beetroot to this dish it stains the rice with an alarming (in a good way) magenta hue. Even more alarming is the tasty combination of sweet beetroot with creamy goat's cheese and crunchy roasted walnuts. If you don't have time to roast the beetroot you can use tinned.

PREPARATION TIME: 20 MINUTES
COOKING TIME: 1 HOUR
SERVES: 6

3 fresh beetroot (beets), scrubbed
    and each cut into 8 wedges
80 ml (2½ fl oz/⅓ cup) olive oil
50 g (1¾ oz) butter
1 onion, finely chopped
4 garlic cloves, finely chopped
330 g (11½ oz/1½ cups)
    arborio rice
125 ml (4 fl oz/½ cup) white wine

1 litre (35 fl oz/4 cups)
    hot chicken stock
1 tablespoon marjoram or oregano,
    chopped
125 g (4½ oz/1 cup) roughly
    chopped walnuts, roasted
100 g (3½ oz) goat's cheese, to serve
rocket (arugula) leaves, to serve

Preheat the oven to 200°C (400°F/Gas 6). Wrap the beetroot in a foil parcel and roast in the oven for 30–40 minutes, or until the beetroot can be pierced easily with a sharp knife but are still firm. When cool enough to handle, slice each beetroot into 8 wedges.

Meanwhile, heat the olive oil and the butter in a large saucepan over medium–low heat. Add the onion and garlic and cook until the onion is translucent. Add the rice and stir to ensure every grain is well coated in the oil. Add the wine and stir gently until all of the wine has evaporated.

Add 125 ml (4 fl oz/½ cup) of the stock to the risotto and stir gently until the liquid has been completely absorbed. Continue to add the stock ½ cup at a time, continually stirring and ensuring the stock has been absorbed before adding more, about 5–8 minutes each time. After 750 ml (26 fl oz/3 cups) of the stock has been added, add the roasted beetroot segments and marjoram or oregano. Add the remaining stock and continue stirring until the rice is tender.

Divide the risotto between serving bowls and top with a generous scattering of walnuts, crumbled goat's cheese and some rocket leaves.

Bejewelled wild rice and risoni salad

This salad is as beautiful on the plate as it is to the palate, making it the perfect addition to any dinner table or picnic blanket. If pomegranates aren't in season, you can substitute any sweet and tangy red fruit, such as grapes, strawberries or even dried cranberries.

PREPARATION TIME: 15 MINUTES + COOLING TIME
COOKING TIME: 50 MINUTES
SERVES: 4

190 g (6¾ oz/1 cup) wild rice
220 g (7¾ oz) risoni pasta
2 zucchini (courgettes), halved lengthways,
    then sliced into 5 mm (⅛ inch) strips
75 g (2¾ oz/½ cup) sunflower seeds, lightly toasted
25 g (1 oz/½ cup) finely chopped mint
½ cup pomegranate seeds
1 tablespoon finely grated lemon zest
60 ml (2 fl oz/¼ cup) lemon juice
2 tablespoons olive oil

Fill a saucepan with 1 litre (35 fl oz/4 cups) water and bring to the boil. Add the wild rice, reduce the heat to low and cook for about 40 minutes, or until the rice is just cracked. Fluff with a fork and set aside to cool.

Cook the risoni in a saucepan of boiling salted water for about 7 minutes (it should be a little underdone, as it will continue to cook after you remove it from the heat), then drain and set aside to cool.

Steam the zucchini in a steamer over a saucepan of boiling water for 2–3 minutes, or until slightly underdone (it will continue to soften once removed from the heat).

In a large bowl, combine the zucchini with the wild rice, risoni, sunflower seeds, mint and pomegranate seeds.

In a separate bowl, mix together the lemon zest, lemon juice and olive oil and season with sea salt and freshly ground black pepper. Add to the salad and toss to combine. Serve at room temperature.

Artwork by
Tai Snaith
watercolour on paper

Fig, fried eggplant and poached chicken salad

The shapes and flavours in this salad give it a distinctively feminine edge, with the subtle perfume of the figs, the curves of the eggplant and the delicateness of the poached chicken.

PREPARATION TIME: 20 MINUTES + COOLING TIME
COOKING TIME: 30 MINUTES
SERVES: 2

70 ml (2¼ fl oz) olive oil
2 onions, thinly sliced into rings
70 ml (2¼ fl oz) balsamic vinegar
4 dried figs, roughly chopped
1 small eggplant (aubergine), halved lengthways, then into 3 mm (⅛ inch) thick wedges
60 ml (2 fl oz/¼ cup) chicken stock

40 g (1½ oz/¼ cup) sunflower seeds, lightly toasted
2 chicken breast fillets
100 g (3½ oz) rocket (arugula)
1 small Lebanese (short) cucumber, halved lengthways and thinly sliced on the diagonal
crusty bread, to serve

Heat 2 tablespoons of the olive oil in a frying pan over medium–low heat. Add the onion and cook for 5 minutes, then add 2 tablespoons of the balsamic vinegar and the figs and cook for a further 5 minutes, or until the onion and fig start to caramelise. Add the eggplant and chicken stock and cook, covered, for 8–10 minutes, or until the eggplant softens. Toss through the sunflower seeds. Remove from the heat and set aside to cool.

Meanwhile, add the chicken breasts to a saucepan of boiling water. Reduce the heat to medium–low and simmer for 10 minutes, or until the chicken is just cooked through. Remove the chicken from the water immediately and set aside. Be careful not to cook the chicken for too long or leave it sitting in the water as this will dry it out. Set aside to rest for 5 minutes before slicing thinly on the diagonal.

Mix together the rocket and cucumber in a large serving bowl. Layer over the chicken slices and eggplant mixture. In a small bowl, combine the remaining olive oil and balsamic vinegar and toss through the salad. This salad can be eaten warm or at room temperature.

Artwork by
Rosalind Monks
pen, ink and digital media

Cauliflower cheese

Almost any vegetable is appealing covered in a creamy white sauce and topped with bubbling golden cheese, but the sweet and juicy nature of cauliflower makes it exceptionally good. This white sauce recipe is souped up with cloves, parsley and other herbs and spices, but for a simpler sauce you can use the version in the lasagne recipe on page 94.

PREPARATION TIME: 25 MINUTES + 15 MINUTES INFUSING
COOKING TIME: 40 MINUTES
SERVES: 4

600 ml (21 fl oz) milk
1 small onion, halved
1 bay leaf
10 whole cloves
6 whole black peppercorns
4 parsley stalks
60 g (2¼ oz) butter
60 g (2¼ oz) plain (all-purpose) flour
1 teaspoon dijon or English mustard

100 g (3½ oz/1 cup) grated
  tasty cheddar cheese
100 g (3½ oz/¾ cup) finely grated
  parmesan cheese
800 g–1 kg (1 lb 12 oz–2 lb 4 oz)
  cauliflower, cut into florets
1 lemon, cut into wedges, to serve
  (optional)

Preheat the oven to 200°C (400°F/Gas 6). Put the milk, onion, bay leaf, cloves, peppercorns and parsley stalks in a large saucepan. Bring just to the boil, then remove from the heat and allow to infuse for 15 minutes. Strain to remove the herbs and spices. Set the milk mixture aside and keep warm.

Melt the butter in a saucepan over medium–low heat. Add the flour and whisk together (this mixture is called a 'roux'). Cook the roux for 1–2 minutes, stirring with a wooden spoon until golden. Add the milk, a little at a time, whisking constantly to thoroughly combine and prevent the mixture from becoming lumpy. Once all of the milk has been incorporated and the sauce is smooth, reduce the heat to low and cook for a further 5–10 minutes, stirring, until the sauce thickly coats the back of the wooden spoon. Remove from the heat, then whisk in the mustard, two-thirds of the cheddar cheese and one-third of the parmesan. Season with sea salt and freshly ground black pepper.

Meanwhile, steam or boil the cauliflower until just tender, about 3 minutes — it should still have a bit of bite to it. Drain and arrange the cauliflower in a 20 x 30 cm (8 x 12 inch) baking dish. Cover with the cheese sauce, top with the remaining cheeses and season with pepper. Bake in the oven for 10–15 minutes, or until golden. Serve this dish with some lemon wedges to cut through the cheesiness, and steamed green vegetables or a fresh salad on the side.

Artwork by
Haw
digital illustration

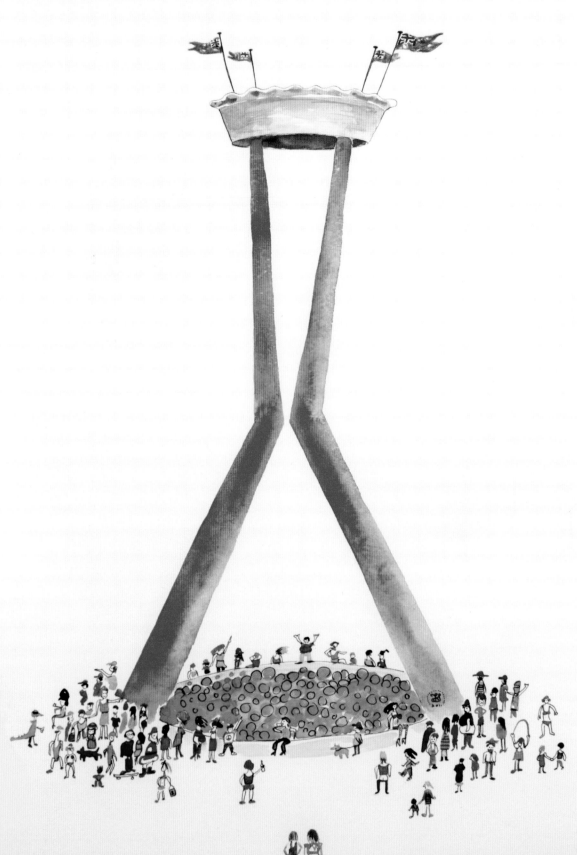

Classic beef pie

There's nothing more Australian than a dog's eye (meat pie) with a coldie (beer) on a scorching summer's day. This take on the classic hearty Australian 'meat poi' is fragrant with fresh herbs and orange rind. Don't forget the dead horse (tomato sauce)!

PREPARATION TIME: 30 MINUTES
 + 2 HOURS CHILLING FOR SHORTCRUST PASTRY
COOKING TIME: 2 HOURS
SERVES: 6

700 g (1 lb 9 oz) beef chuck steak, trimmed and cut into 1.5 cm (⅝ inch) cubes
2 tablespoons plain (all-purpose) flour
60 ml (2 fl oz/¼ cup) olive oil
1 tablespoon butter
2 large onions, finely chopped
2 garlic cloves, chopped
250 ml (9 fl oz/1 cup) red wine
250 ml (9 fl oz/1 cup) beef stock
1 tablespoon worcestershire sauce
1 small rosemary sprig

1 strip orange rind, white pith removed
1 bay leaf
milk, to glaze

SHORTCRUST PASTRY
350 g (12 oz/2⅓ cups) plain (all-purpose) flour
a pinch of salt
150 g (5½ oz) cold butter, cubed
1 egg, plus 2 egg yolks, lightly beaten
1 tablespoon iced water

To make the shortcrust pastry, combine the flour and salt in a bowl. Using a food processor or your fingertips, process or rub together the butter and flour, until the mixture resembles fine breadcrumbs. Add the egg and egg yolks and process just long enough to bring the dough together, adding a little iced water if necessary.

Break off two-thirds of the dough to use as the pie base and roll into a ball. Roll the remaining one-third into a ball — this will be used to make the pie 'lid'. Flatten both balls slightly into disc shapes, wrap in plastic wrap and refrigerate for at least 2 hours.

Meanwhile, to make the filling, put the beef and flour in a plastic bag and shake to coat the beef, then remove the meat from the bag and shake off any excess flour. Heat 1 tablespoon of the olive oil in a large saucepan over medium–high heat. Add the beef, in batches, and cook until brown on all sides, then remove from the pan once cooked and set aside.

Artwork by
Tai Snaith
watercolour on paper

CONTINUED ➙

Without washing the pan, add the remaining oil and the butter over low heat, then add the onion and garlic and cook until translucent, about 8 minutes. Return the beef to the pan with the wine, stock, worcestershire sauce, rosemary, orange rind, bay leaf and 375 ml (13 fl oz/1½ cups) water. Cover and cook gently over low heat for at least 1 hour, or until the meat is very tender. Season with sea salt and freshly ground black pepper, and set aside to cool. Remove and discard the rosemary sprig, orange rind and bay leaf.

Remove the pastry from the refrigerator 20 minutes before you wish to start rolling. Preheat the oven to 200°C (400°F/Gas 6). Grease a 23 cm (9 inch) round pie dish. Roll out the dough discs between two sheets of baking paper, so each is 3 mm (⅛ inch) thick, dusting the surfaces with flour if necessary to prevent them from sticking. Return the smaller pastry circle to the refrigerator.

Line the pie dish with the larger pastry circle, trimming to fit. Line the pastry shell with baking paper and top with pastry weights (you can also use uncooked rice, lentils or beans, but will either need to discard these afterwards or reserve them for your next pastry). Blind-bake the pastry for 15 minutes, then remove from the oven and remove the paper and weights.

Add the cooled meat to the pastry shell and top with the smaller sheet of pastry, rolling the edges to form a crust. Gently pierce the top of the pie with a fork several times, then brush with milk. Bake the pie in the oven for 20–25 minutes, or until the pastry is golden. Cut into wedges and serve.

Corned beef and friends

This is our favourite one of Mum's meals, with its combination of classic corned beef, buttery beetroot, fresh steamed greens and hollandaise sauce with cracked potatoes. There's nothing more comforting than corned beef and vegetables, but we like to call our version corned beef and 'friends' because these accompaniments were made for each other. A corned beef–beetroot–mustard sandwich the next day will win your heart a second time!

PREPARATION TIME: 45 MINUTES
COOKING TIME: 1 HOUR 10 MINUTES
SERVES: 6

1 kg (2 lb 4 oz) corned beef
1 onion, peeled
6 whole cloves
1 teaspoon whole black peppercorns
lemon wedges, to serve
cracked potatoes (page 116),
    to serve
your favourite mustards, such as
    hot English, dijon or wholegrain,
    to serve

BUTTERY BEETROOT
50 g (1¾ oz) butter
4 beetroot (beets), peeled and
    grated
2 tablespoons finely chopped dill
60 ml (2 fl oz/¼ cup) lemon juice
1 tablespoon plain (all-purpose)
    flour
125 ml (4 fl oz/½ cup) chicken stock
2 teaspoons sea salt
1 teaspoon freshly ground black
    pepper

HOLLANDAISE SAUCE
3 egg yolks, at room temperature
75 g (2¾ oz) unsalted butter, cubed,
    at room temperature
1 tablespoon lemon juice, or to taste

To prepare the corned beef, place the beef in a large saucepan or stockpot and cover with water. Bring to the boil, then discard the water to reduce the saltiness of the meat. Cover the beef with fresh water, add the onion, cloves and peppercorns and bring to the boil over high heat. Reduce the heat to low, cover, and simmer for about 1 hour, or until the beef is tender — you may need to add more water to the pan during cooking so the beef is covered at all times.

Meanwhile, to make the buttery beetroot, heat the butter in a large saucepan over medium–low heat. Add the beetroot and cook for about 5 minutes, stirring occasionally. Add the dill and lemon juice, reduce the heat to low, cover, and cook for 20 minutes. Sprinkle the flour into the pan and cook without stirring for a further 5 minutes. Mix in the stock and cook for a further 10 minutes, stirring occasionally. Season with sea salt and freshly ground black pepper.

CONTINUED →

To make the hollandaise sauce, place the egg yolks and 2 tablespoons water in a heatproof bowl over a saucepan of gently simmering water, making sure the base of the bowl does not touch the water — too much heat will curdle the mixture. Whisk the mixture constantly for 3 minutes, or until it is thick and pale, has doubled in volume and a ribbon trail forms when the whisk is lifted. Add the butter, a cube at a time, whisking constantly after each addition until it melts. The cooked sauce should have the consistency of lightly whisked thickened cream. Remove the bowl from the pan and whisk in the lemon juice, to taste, then season with salt and pepper.

Serve slices of corned beef with the cracked potatoes, buttery beetroot, hollandaise sauce, some steamed greens, a wedge of lemon and mustard.

Artwork by
Kitty Horton
acrylic on paper

Crunchy polenta and fresh tomato sauce

These crunchy golden squares can be served with any pasta sauce. They can be baked or fried. If you have excess, wrap up the uncooked squares and pop them in the freezer, ready for another quick meal.

PREPARATION TIME: 30 MINUTES + 30 MINUTES REFRIGERATION
COOKING TIME: 1 HOUR 20 MINUTES
SERVES: 4

CRUNCHY POLENTA
1 litre (35 fl oz/4 cups) vegetable
  or chicken stock
380 g (13½ oz/2 cups) polenta
  (cornmeal)
20 g (¾ oz) butter
100 g (3½ oz/¾ cup) finely grated
  parmesan cheese, plus extra
  to serve
olive oil, for frying

TOMATO SAUCE
2 x 400 g (14 oz) tins whole
  tomatoes, roughly chopped
40 g (1½ oz) butter
1 large onion, chopped
1 teaspoon salt
1 teaspoon sugar

To make the tomato sauce, combine all of the ingredients in a large saucepan and bring to the boil. Reduce the heat to low and simmer for 30 minutes. Remove from the heat and keep warm or reheat gently before serving.

To make the crunchy polenta, lightly grease a 23 x 30 cm (9 x 12 inch) baking dish. Combine the stock and 500 ml (17 fl oz/2 cups) water in a large saucepan and bring to the boil. Add the polenta in a steady stream, stirring as you pour. Continue to stir over medium–low heat for about 20 minutes, or until the polenta is cooked (when it is ready it will start to come away from the sides of the pan). Stir in the butter and parmesan and season with sea salt and freshly ground black pepper. Pour the polenta into the prepared dish and smooth the top — it should be about 1.5 cm (⅝ inch) thick. Refrigerate for about 30 minutes, or until set. Cut into squares.

There are two ways to cook the polenta. You can fry it — heat enough olive oil to come 1 cm (½ inch) up the side of a frying pan over medium–high heat and fry the squares for about 5 minutes on each side, or until crispy. Alternatively, you can bake it — arrange the polenta on a lightly greased baking tray and bake in a preheated 200°C (400°F/Gas 6) oven for about 30 minutes, or until crispy.

Serve the polenta topped with the tomato sauce and some extra parmesan.

Artwork by
Riki Salam
digital illustration

Fattoush with lime and black pepper-crusted lamb backstrap

This brightly coloured and textured salad teams well with most roast meats, particularly this peppery, citrusy pepper lamb. Its vibrancy and freshness make it a great meal for warmer weather and outdoor dining. It is easily transportable too, as the lamb can be served hot or cold.

PREPARATION TIME: 20 MINUTES+ 30 MINUTES REFRIGERATION
COOKING TIME: 10 MINUTES
SERVES: 4

2 cups shredded cos (romaine) lettuce
2 Lebanese (short) cucumbers, halved lengthways, seeds removed and diced
2 tomatoes, finely diced
3 radishes, halved and thinly sliced
1 large piece pitta bread, toasted and broken into small pieces
4 spring onions (scallions), thinly sliced
2 tablespoons finely chopped mint
15 g (½ oz/½ cup) finely chopped flat-leaf (Italian) parsley

60 ml (2 fl oz/¼ cup) extra virgin olive oil
2 tablespoons lemon juice
½ teaspoon sweet paprika

LIME AND PEPPER-CRUSTED LAMB
finely grated zest of 4 limes
1 tablespoon lime juice
1 tablespoon whole black peppercorns, crushed
1 tablespoon olive oil, plus extra for cooking
2 lamb backstraps (each about 18 cm/7 inches long)

To make the lime and pepper-crusted lamb, combine the lime zest and juice, crushed peppercorns and olive oil in a bowl. Roll the lamb in this mixture to coat, then place on a plate and refrigerate for 30 minutes.

To make the fattoush, combine the lettuce, cucumber, tomato, radish, bread, spring onion, mint and parsley in a large bowl. In a separate small bowl, mix together the olive oil, lemon juice, sweet paprika, sea salt and freshly ground black pepper to taste. Add this dressing to the fattoush and toss well.

Heat a little extra olive oil in a large frying pan over medium–high heat. Add the lamb and cook on each side for 2–3 minutes, or until cooked to your liking. Remove from the pan, wrap in foil and allow to rest for 5 minutes before slicing on the diagonal. Serve the lamb hot, cold or warm with a generous pile of salad.

Artwork by
Vexta
mixed media

Spiced tomato prawns with avocado and cucumber salsa

This dish is fresh and fragrant — the prawns are cooked with star anise, coriander and tomatoes and served with a spicy avocado and cucumber salsa. The rice is perfect for soaking up all the exotic juices! To cook the rice we swear by our '20-minute method'. Crucial to this method is not lifting the lid of the saucepan during cooking — not even for a peek!

PREPARATION TIME: 25 MINUTES
COOKING TIME: 30 MINUTES
SERVES: 4

200 g (7 oz/1 cup) jasmine
   or basmati rice
2 tablespoons grapeseed oil
4 garlic cloves, finely chopped
1 red bird's eye chilli, seeded and
   thinly sliced
1 teaspoon tomato paste
   (concentrated purée)
1 tablespoon caster (superfine)
   sugar
1 star anise
500 g (1 lb 2 oz/about 14) raw
   prawns (shrimp), peeled,
   deveined with tails left intact
3 tomatoes, diced
80 ml (2½ fl oz/⅓ cup) fish sauce

3 spring onions (scallions),
   chopped
15 g (½ oz/¼ cup) chopped
   coriander (cilantro) leaves,
   to serve

AVOCADO AND CUCUMBER SALSA
1 large avocado, peeled, stone
   removed and cut into cubes
1 Lebanese (short) cucumber, diced
20 g (¾ oz/⅓ cup) chopped
   coriander (cilantro) leaves
1 tablespoon olive oil
1 tablespoon lime juice
½ teaspoon caster (superfine)
   sugar

To make the avocado and cucumber salsa, combine the avocado, cucumber and coriander in a bowl. In a separate bowl, combine the olive oil, lime juice and sugar; season well. Add the dressing to the avocado mixture and toss to coat.

To cook the rice, combine it with 310 ml (10¾ fl oz/1¼ cups) water in a saucepan and bring to the boil. As soon as the water starts to boil, reduce the heat to the lowest possible setting, cover the pan with a tight-fitting lid, and simmer for 20 minutes. Once cooked, remove the lid and fluff the rice with a fork.

Meanwhile, heat the grapeseed oil in a large wok or heavy-based frying pan over medium–high heat. Add the garlic and chilli and cook for 1 minute. Add the tomato paste, sugar, star anise and 60 ml (2 fl oz/¼ cup) water, and stir until the sugar has dissolved. Add the prawns and cook for 1–2 minutes, then add the tomato, fish sauce, spring onion and another ¼ cup water and cook for 3–4 minutes, or until the prawns are just cooked; season to taste. Remove the prawns to a plate, then increase the heat and continue to cook the sauce for 2–3 minutes. Return the prawns to the wok, stir well then remove from the heat.

Arrange some prawns over a bed of rice, sprinkle with coriander and serve with a heap of salsa.

Artwork by
Victoria Topping
digital illustration

Lasagne

Lasagne is so widely consumed and adored around the world that each home has their unique take on it — the bolognaise component alone may include variations of red wine, white wine, stock, milk, tomatoes, sofrito and cured meats for flavouring. This is our mum's lasagne recipe, with red wine in the bolognaise and a simple béchamel sauce.

PREPARATION TIME: 30 MINUTES
COOKING TIME: 2 HOURS 10 MINUTES
SERVES: 6

250 g (9 oz) fresh or dried
    lasagne sheets
100 g (3½ oz/¾ cup) finely grated
    parmesan cheese

BOLOGNAISE
60 ml (2 fl oz/¼ cup) olive oil
1 large onion, finely chopped
3 garlic cloves, finely chopped
50 g (1¾ oz) pancetta or bacon,
    finely chopped
1 kg (2 lb 4 oz) minced (ground) beef
2 tablespoons plain (all-purpose) flour
125 ml (4 fl oz/½ cup) red wine
2 x 400 g (14 oz) tins whole tomatoes
2 tablespoons tomato paste
    (concentrated purée)
1 teaspoon sugar
1 bay leaf
1 thyme sprig

BÉCHAMEL SAUCE
75 g (2¾ oz) butter
75 g (2¾ oz/½ cup) plain
    (all-purpose) flour
1 litre (35 fl oz/4 cups)
    warm milk
¼ teaspoon freshly grated
    nutmeg

To make the bolognaise, heat the olive oil in a large saucepan over medium–low heat. Add the onion and garlic and cook for 5 minutes, then add the pancetta and cook for a further 5 minutes, or until the onion has softened. Increase the heat a little, add the beef and fry, stirring and breaking up any larger bits of meat, until browned. Add the flour and cook, stirring well, until all of the liquid has been absorbed. Add the wine and cook until the liquid evaporates, stirring regularly.

Add the tomatoes, tomato paste, sugar, bay leaf, thyme and 170 ml (5½ fl oz/⅔ cup) water to the pan. Season well with sea salt and freshly ground black pepper, cover, and simmer over low heat for at least 45 minutes, or until the sauce has reduced and thickened, stirring occasionally (making sure to stir into the corners of the saucepan to avoid the bolognaise sticking and burning). The longer you cook it, the deeper the flavour.

CONTINUED ➤➤

Artwork by
Josh Rufford
mixed media on wood

To make the béchamel sauce, melt the butter in a saucepan over medium–low heat. Add the flour and whisk together (this mixture is called a 'roux'). Cook the roux for about 1–2 minutes, stirring with a wooden spoon until golden. Add the milk, a little at a time, whisking constantly to thoroughly combine and prevent the mixture from becoming lumpy. Once all of the milk has been incorporated and the sauce is smooth, reduce the heat to low and cook for a further 5–10 minutes, stirring until the sauce thickly coats the back of a wooden spoon. Stir in the nutmeg and season to taste with sea salt and freshly ground black pepper.

Preheat the oven to 180°C (350°F/Gas 4). Lightly grease a 20 x 30 cm (8 x 12 inch) baking dish. Spread one-third of the bolognaise in the base of the dish. Top with a layer of lasagne sheets, then spread over one-third of the béchamel sauce. Repeat this layering twice more, finishing with a layer of béchamel sauce. Scatter over the parmesan cheese and bake for about 45 minutes, or until the cheese has browned and the pasta is cooked.

Cut the lasagne into slices, to serve, and get ready to feel content.

Meatballs of the world: Italian, Greek and Moroccan

It's the meatball Olympics and in the running are Italy, Greece and Morocco. Each country has put some of their biggest flavours forward: Italy with parmesan and parsley, Greece with feta and mint, and Morocco with cinnamon and honey. You decide the winner! Although we've recommended what to serve the meatballs with, you can mix and match between rice, couscous, different types of pasta, or even some crusty bread or a bun for a meatball sub.

PREPARATION TIME: 30 MINUTES
COOKING TIME: 40 MINUTES
SERVES: 4

GREEK MEATBALLS

- 500 g (1 lb 2 oz) minced (ground) beef
- 2 spring onions (scallions), thinly sliced
- 1 teaspoon finely grated lemon zest
- 2 teaspoons finely chopped oregano
- 100 g (3½ oz/⅔ cup) crumbled feta cheese
- 30 g (1 oz/½ cup) fresh or dry breadcrumbs
- 1 egg, lightly beaten
- 2 tablespoons olive oil, for frying

ITALIAN MEATBALLS

- 500 g (1 lb 2 oz) minced (ground) beef
- 15 g (½ oz/½ cup) finely chopped flat-leaf (Italian) parsley
- 1 onion, finely chopped
- 30 g (1 oz/½ cup) fresh or dry breadcrumbs
- 1 egg, lightly beaten
- 2 tablespoons olive oil, for frying
- 220 g (7¾ oz) risoni pasta
- 30 g (1 oz/½ cup) basil leaves, torn, to serve
- 35 g (1¼ oz/¼ cup) finely grated parmesan cheese, plus extra to serve

MOROCCAN MEATBALLS

- 500 g (1 lb 2 oz) minced (ground) beef
- 1 onion, grated
- ¾ teaspoon fennel seeds, toasted
- ¾ teaspoon ground cinnamon
- ¾ teaspoon ground cumin
- 30 g (1 oz/½ cup) fresh or dry breadcrumbs
- 1 egg, lightly beaten
- 2 tablespoons olive oil, for frying
- 1 cinnamon stick or ¾ teaspoon ground cinnamon (optional)
- 2 tablespoons honey (optional)
- 25 g (1 oz/½ cup) chopped coriander (cilantro) leaves, to serve

TOMATO SAUCE

- 40 g (1½ oz) butter
- 1 onion, cut in half
- 2 x 400 g (14 oz) tins whole tomatoes, roughly chopped
- 1 teaspoon caster (superfine) sugar

For all varieties of meatballs, combine all of the ingredients up to, but not including, the olive oil, in a large bowl and mix well — your hands are the best tool for this job. Roll the mixture into small balls and set aside on a plate.

Heat the olive oil in a large frying pan over medium–high heat and fry the meatballs for 2–3 minutes, turning to brown evenly on all sides — they do not need to be cooked through at this stage as they will finish cooking in the sauce.

To make the tomato sauce, put the butter, onion, tomatoes and sugar in a saucepan. Season with sea salt and freshly ground black pepper and place over medium–high heat. Bring to the boil, then reduce the heat to low and simmer for 20 minutes.

If you are making Greek meatballs, add the meatballs to the sauce and continue to simmer for a further 10 minutes, or until the meatballs are cooked through and serve with rice.

If you are making Italian meatballs, add the risoni and meatballs to the sauce and continue to simmer for a further 7–10 minutes, or until the meatballs are cooked through and the risoni is just undercooked — it will continue to cook after it's removed from the heat. Serve the risoni and meatballs topped with torn basil leaves and parmesan cheese.

If you are making the sauce to serve with Morrocan meatballs, add the cinnamon to the pan with the sauce. After simmering for 20 minutes stir in the honey, add the meatballs and cook for a further 10 minutes, or until cooked through. Serve with couscous and top with fresh coriander.

Artwork by
Femke de Jong
digital illustration

Mexican fish cakes with salsa

Hand-cut chunks give these fragrant fish cakes their character, and are complemented by a sweet and spicy tomato salsa. We recommend making the salsa in large quantities, as it's a simple and fresh accompaniment to many dishes. Try it with zucchini fritters (page 140) or salt and pepper squid (page 124).

PREPARATION TIME: 30 MINUTES
COOKING TIME: 10 MINUTES
SERVES: 4

FISH CAKES

1 kg (2 lb 4 oz) skinless, boneless white fish fillets, finely chopped
1 egg
2 garlic cloves, finely chopped
1 tablespoon finely grated ginger
4 spring onions (scallions), finely chopped
3 tablespoons finely chopped coriander (cilantro) leaves
2 tablespoons finely chopped mint
2 long red chillies, seeded and finely chopped
2 teaspoons finely grated lime zest
1 tablespoon lime juice
grapeseed oil, for frying
lime wedges, to serve

TOMATO SALSA

4 tomatoes, diced
4 spring onions (scallions), thinly sliced
20 g (¾ oz/⅓ cup) chopped coriander (cilantro) leaves
2 tablespoons lime juice
1 tablespoon extra virgin olive oil
½ teaspoon caster (superfine) sugar
¼ teaspoon sea salt

To make the tomato salsa, combine the tomato, spring onion and coriander in a bowl. In a separate bowl, mix together the lime juice, olive oil, sugar and salt. Add to the tomatoes and mix well to combine. Refrigerate until ready to serve.

To make the fish cakes, combine the fish, egg, garlic, ginger, spring onion, coriander, mint, chilli and lime zest and juice in a large bowl. Mix well and season with sea salt and freshly ground black pepper. Using wet hands, shape the mixture into patties and set aside.

Pour enough grapeseed oil into a large frying pan so it is about 1 cm (½ inch) deep and place over medium–high heat. Add the fish cakes and cook for 2 minutes on each side, or until just cooked through. Serve the fish cakes with a mound of tomato salsa and a wedge of lime.

Artwork by
Adam Oehlers
pencil on paper

Yoghurt lamb with masala potatoes and spicy fried cabbage

This fragrant lamb curry is flavoured with lots of spice love in the form of ginger, paprika, mint and coriander. The tangy lemon potatoes and sweet and spicy cabbage make for a beautifully balanced meal that is sure to satisfy any mid-week curry cravings.

PREPARATION TIME: 40 MINUTES + 1 HOUR MARINATING TIME
COOKING TIME: 1 HOUR 20 MINUTES
SERVES: 4

YOGHURT LAMB

- 600 g (1 lb 5 oz) lamb shoulder, cut into 2 cm (¾ inch) cubes
- 190 g (6¾ oz/⅔ cup) plain yoghurt
- 60 g (2¼ oz/¼ cup) tomato paste (concentrated purée)
- 3 garlic cloves, finely chopped
- 1 tablespoon finely grated ginger
- ½ teaspoon chilli powder
- 1 teaspoon salt
- 2 tablespoons grapeseed oil
- 1 teaspoon sweet paprika
- 1 teaspoon garam masala
- 2 tablespoons chopped coriander (cilantro) leaves
- 2 tablespoons chopped mint
- finely chopped red chilli, to serve

MASALA POTATOES

- 2 tablespoons grapeseed oil
- 1 onion, chopped
- 2 garlic cloves, finely chopped
- 1 teaspoon finely grated ginger
- 1 teaspoon black mustard seeds
- 1 teaspoon ground cumin
- 2 teaspoons ground turmeric
- 1 tablespoon coriander (cilantro) stems, chopped
- 4 all-purpose potatoes, washed and cut into 1 cm (½ inch) cubes
- 1 tablespoon lemon juice
- 1 teaspoon sea salt
- 2 tablespoons coriander (cilantro) leaves, chopped

SPICY FRIED CABBAGE

- 1 tablespoon grapeseed oil
- ¼ green cabbage, roughly chopped
- 1 long green chilli, seeded and finely chopped
- ½ teaspoon salt
- ½ teaspoon sugar

To make the yoghurt lamb, combine the lamb, yoghurt, tomato paste, garlic, ginger, chilli powder and salt in a bowl. Cover and refrigerate for at least 1 hour to marinate.

Heat the grapeseed oil in a large frying pan over medium–high heat. Add the paprika and garam masala and cook for 1 minute, stirring constantly, then add the lamb and marinade and stir to coat the meat in the spices. Add 170 ml (5½ fl oz/ ⅔ cup) water, cover, reduce the heat to low and simmer for 45–60 minutes, or until the lamb is tender. Remove from the heat, stir through the coriander and mint and season to taste.

CONTINUED →→

Artwork by
Riki Salam
gouache and ink on watercolour paper

Meanwhile, make the masala potatoes. Heat the grapeseed oil in a large saucepan over medium heat. Add the onion and fry for 2–3 minutes, or until lightly browned. Add the garlic and ginger and cook for a further 1 minute. Add the mustard seeds, cumin, turmeric and coriander stems and cook until the mustard seeds start to pop. Add the potato and stir to coat in the spices, adding a few tablespoons of water to prevent the mixture sticking. Cover, reduce the heat to low and cook for about 15 minutes, or until the potatoes are soft but still firm. Add the lemon juice and salt to taste, then stir through the coriander leaves. Keep warm until ready to serve.

To make the spicy fried cabbage, heat the grapeseed oil in a frying pan over medium–high heat. Add the cabbage and cook for 2–3 minutes, or until the cabbage has softened. Add the chilli, salt and sugar and stir to combine. Cover and cook for 3–4 minutes, or until the cabbage softens. Keep warm until ready to serve.

Serve the lamb, masala potatoes and cabbage together with some extra chilli, plain yoghurt and as much chutney as you can lay your hands on.

Moroccan chicken with couscous

This dish is sweetened with honey and spiced with the Moroccan flavours of cumin, cinnamon and ginger. You can substitute chicken thighs with any other cut — the fattier the cut the richer the flavour. Buttery couscous is the perfect match for soaking up the sweet sauce, but you can substitute steamed rice or quinoa.

PREPARATION TIME: 20 MINUTES
COOKING TIME: 40 MINUTES
SERVES: 6

6 chicken thigh fillets
2 tablespoons olive oil, plus extra for frying
40 g (1½ oz) butter
1 large brown onion, halved and thinly sliced
2 garlic cloves, finely chopped
1 teaspoon ground ginger
1 teaspoon ground coriander
1 teaspoon ground cinnamon
1 teaspoon ground cumin
½ teaspoon cayenne pepper
2 x 400 g (14 oz) tins whole tomatoes,
    roughly chopped
60 g (2¼ oz/¼ cup) honey
chopped coriander (cilantro) leaves, to serve

COUSCOUS
2 teaspoons olive oil
380 g (13½ oz/2 cups) couscous
40 g (1½ oz) butter
1 tablespoon finely grated lemon zest (optional)
1 tablespoon sesame seeds, lightly toasted (optional)

To make the Moroccan chicken, rub the chicken thighs with sea salt and freshly ground black pepper and set aside. Heat the olive oil and butter in a saucepan over medium–low heat. Add the onion and garlic and cook for 3–4 minutes, or until the onion has softened. Add the ground ginger, coriander, cinnamon, cumin and cayenne pepper and cook for a further 1–2 minutes, stirring until fragrant. Add the tomatoes and stir well to combine. Bring to the boil, then reduce the heat and simmer for 15 minutes. Stir in the honey and simmer for a further 2 minutes.

CONTINUED ➔➤

In a large frying pan, heat 1 tablespoon of the extra oil over medium heat. Add the chicken and cook for 2–3 minutes on all sides to brown. Add the tomato mixture to the pan and simmer over low heat until the chicken is just cooked through, about 7 minutes.

To make the couscous, combine the olive oil and 500 ml (17 fl oz/2 cups) water in a saucepan and bring to the boil. Stir in the couscous, then remove from the heat, cover, and set aside for 3 minutes. Return the pan to low heat, add the butter and mix through with a fork to fluff the grains. Continue to cook for a further 2 minutes, stirring regularly so it doesn't catch in the pan and burn. Remove from the heat and mix through the lemon zest and sesame seeds, if using.

Pile mounds of the buttery couscous onto plates, top with some chicken and a generous amount of sauce and sprinkle with coriander leaves.

Artwork by
Sarah Dennis
digital illustration

Seafood paella

Paella is a great party dish, a single-pan banquet that you can pack with a variety of ingredients, such as mussels, fish, chicken, rabbit and chorizo. We've enjoyed paella made with yabbies that were caught in a dam after a farm trip out West, for Christmas with local sand crab, and cooked on the beach over a fire with the catch of the day. To ensure you get the characteristic rice 'crust' on the bottom of your paella, it is important that you resist the urge to stir it during the final stage of cooking.

PREPARATION TIME: 25 MINUTES + 20 MINUTES FOR SOAKING SAFFRON
COOKING TIME: 45 MINUTES
SERVES: 8

60 ml (2 fl oz/¼ cup) olive oil
1 onion, finely chopped
2 garlic cloves, finely chopped
1 chorizo, diced
3 tomatoes, peeled and chopped
1 red capsicum (pepper), chopped
400 g (14 oz/2 cups) calasparra rice (or use risotto or basmati rice if unavailable)
10 saffron threads, soaked in 1 tablespoon of water for 20 minutes
1 tablespoon smoked paprika

250 ml (9 fl oz/1 cup) fish or chicken stock
250 ml (9 fl oz/1 cup) white wine
3 squid tubes, sliced into rings
750 g (1 lb 10 oz) raw prawns (shrimp), peeled, deveined with tails left intact
18 fresh black mussels, debearded and washed
200 g (7 oz/1⅓ cups) peas (or use beans cut into 2 cm/¾ inch pieces)
10 g (¼ oz/⅓ cup) chopped flat-leaf (Italian) parsley
lemon or lime wedges, to serve

Heat the olive oil in a paella pan or a large heavy-based frying pan over medium heat. Add the onion and cook for 3–4 minutes, or until translucent. Add the garlic, chorizo, tomato and capsicum and cook for a further 5–8 minutes, or until the tomato breaks down. Add the rice, saffron and paprika and stir for 1 minute to coat the rice.

Add the stock to the pan with the wine and 500 ml (17 fl oz/2 cups) water and stir to combine. Reduce the heat to low and cook, uncovered, for about 15 minutes, or until the stock has reduced and the rice has begun to swell. Scatter over the squid, prawns and mussels, season well with salt and freshly ground black pepper and cook for a further 5 minutes. Add the peas, push the mussels further into the rice and cover with foil. Cook for a further 3–5 minutes, or until the peas are cooked and mussel shells have opened (discard any that don't open). Remove the foil, increase the heat to medium–high, scatter over the parsley and leave to cook for a further 3–5 minutes. Serve with lemon wedges on the side.

Artwork by
Rosalind Monks
ink, paper and digital

Pea and pancetta risotto

This colourful risotto has spinach woven through the creamy grains of rice, sweet peas that burst in your mouth, and chunks of salty pancetta. Risottos require a lot of TLC — be prepared to stand by, wooden spoon in one hand, glass of wine in the other, to nurture it for the 30 minutes it takes to absorb all the liquid.

PREPARATION TIME: 15 MINUTES
COOKING TIME: 40 MINUTES
SERVES: 4

2 tablespoons olive oil
50 g (1¾ oz) butter
1 onion, finely chopped
4 garlic cloves, finely chopped
250 g (9 oz) pancetta, shaved or
    chopped into small chunks
330 g (11½ oz/1½ cups) arborio rice
125 ml (4 fl oz/½ cup) white wine
1 litre (35 fl oz/4 cups) hot chicken stock
250 g (9 oz) fresh or frozen spinach, defrosted and squeezed
    of excess moisture, chopped
155 g (5½ oz/1 cup) fresh or frozen peas
50 g (1¾ oz/⅓ cup) finely grated parmesan cheese,
    plus extra to serve

Heat the olive oil and butter in a saucepan over medium–low heat. Add the onion and garlic and cook for 3–4 minutes, or until the onion is translucent. Add the pancetta and fry for 1–2 minutes to brown, then add the rice and stir to ensure every grain is coated in oil. Add the wine and stir gently until it evaporates.

Add 125 ml (4 fl oz/½ cup) of the hot stock to the pan and stir gently until the liquid has been completely absorbed. Continue to add stock in this way, ½ cup at a time, stirring constantly and ensuring all of the liquid is absorbed before adding more — this will take about 5–8 minutes between each addition.

After 750 ml (26 fl oz/3 cups) of the stock has been added, add the spinach and peas and the remaining stock and stir until the liquid has been absorbed and the rice is tender. Stir through the parmesan, divide between serving bowls and serve immediately with extra parmesan.

Artwork by
David Williams
digital illustration

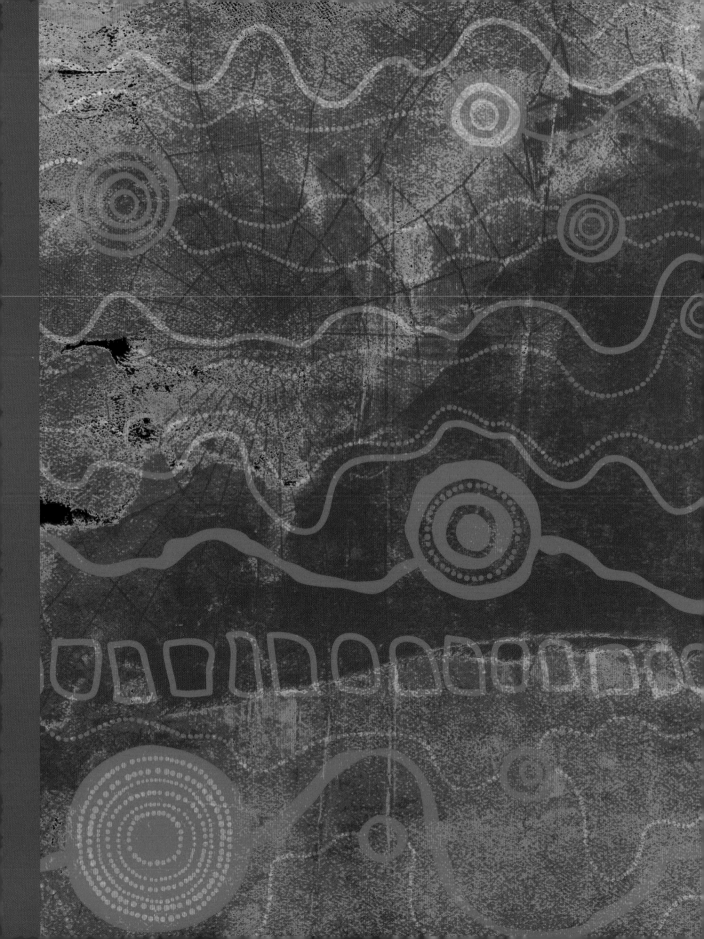

Puy lentil and feta salad

This salad of nutty puy lentils and creamy feta is packed full of liver-cleansing parsley, crunchy cucumber and sweet red onions. Satisfying on its own, it is also a perfect accompaniment to most grilled meats and fish.

PREPARATION TIME: 20 MINUTES + COOLING
COOKING TIME: 15 MINUTES
SERVES: 4–6

210 g (7½ oz/1 cup) puy lentils
1 bay leaf
30 g (1 oz/1 cup) chopped flat-leaf (Italian) parsley
20 g (¾ oz/⅓ cup) finely chopped mint
1 small red onion, finely chopped
1 Lebanese (short) cucumber, diced
150 g (5½ oz) feta cheese, cut into small cubes
2 tablespoons olive oil
2 tablespoons lemon juice
1 tablespoon red wine vinegar

Combine the lentils and bay leaf in a saucepan with 750 ml (26 fl oz/3 cups) water. Bring to the boil, then reduce the heat to low and simmer for about 15 minutes, or until the lentils are tender but firm. Discard the bay leaf, drain the lentils and set aside to cool.

In a large bowl, combine the parsley, mint, onion, cucumber, feta and cooled lentils.

In a separate bowl, combine the olive oil, lemon juice and red wine vinegar and season with sea salt and freshly ground black pepper, to taste. Toss through the lentil salad to coat before serving.

Artwork by
Cam Jones
watercolour on paper

Roasted rolled chicken with pistachio, apricot and lemon stuffing

While living in Brisbane together, we befriended our local butcher to learn some meat cooking tips and tricks. He invited us into his shop one night to learn how to bone and stuff a chicken. The terms were that we had to each bring in a stuffing and he would judge the best. This is Jessie's winning recipe.

PREPARATION TIME: 30 MINUTES + 10 MINUTES SOAKING FOR APRICOTS
COOKING TIME: 1 HOUR + 10 MINUTES RESTING
SERVES: 6

130 g (4¾ oz/¾ cup) dried apricots
50 g (1¾ oz/⅓ cup) pistachio nuts, roughly chopped
50 g (1¾ oz/⅓ cup) finely grated parmesan cheese
40 g (1½ oz/⅓ cup) fresh or dry breadcrumbs
4 spring onions (scallions), chopped
35 g (1¼ oz/¾ cup) chopped coriander (cilantro) leaves
15 g (½ oz/½ cup) chopped flat-leaf (Italian) parsley
½ preserved lemon, flesh discarded and rind finely chopped
1 tablespoon finely grated lemon zest
½ teaspoon ground cumin
2 tablespoons lemon juice
40 g (1½ oz) butter, cubed
1 whole chicken, deboned

Soak the apricots in warm water for 10 minutes, then drain and chop.

Preheat the oven to 180°C (350°F/Gas 4). Lightly grease a baking tray. In a large bowl, mix together the apricots, pistachios, parmesan, breadcrumbs, spring onion, coriander, parsley, preserved lemon, lemon zest and cumin. Add the lemon juice and butter cubes and mix well.

Lay the chicken open, with the inside facing up. Squeeze handfuls of the stuffing together and place in the middle of the chicken. Fold in the top and bottom edges first, then roll up the chicken as tightly as possible. Secure with kitchen string. Place the chicken on the prepared tray and bake for 45–60 minutes. If the chicken looks like it's browning too much on the outside, cover it with foil.

Remove the chicken from the oven, wrap in foil and set aside to rest for about 10 minutes before serving. Remove the string and slice the chicken thickly. Serve with your favourite roast vegetables or salad.

Artwork by
Nadine Sawyer
acrylic on canvas

Seeded mustard roast beef with cracked potatoes and basil tomatoes

This roast has distinguishing little touches that are sure to leave a lasting impression. The beef is smothered in seeded mustard that forms a memorable crust, the basil tomatoes are strikingly sharp from the generous amount of rock salt, and the potatoes are cracked and crunchy.

PREPARATION TIME: 30 MINUTES
COOKING TIME: 1 HOUR + 10 MINUTES RESTING
SERVES: 6

CRACKED POTATOES
olive oil, for greasing
12 small all-purpose potatoes,
   such as desiree
30 g (1 oz) butter
fresh rosemary sprigs

SEEDED MUSTARD ROAST BEEF
1 kg (2 lb 4 oz) beef rib fillet
125 g (4½ oz/½ cup) seeded
   mustard, plus extra for serving

BASIL TOMATOES
10 g (¼ oz/⅓ cup) basil leaves
1 garlic clove
2 teaspoons rock salt
1 tablespoon olive oil
6 ripe tomatoes, cut into wedges
2 teaspoons balsamic vinegar

To make the cracked potatoes, preheat the oven to 200°C (400°F/Gas 6) and grease a baking tray with olive oil. Before baking you need to par-boil the potatoes. Place the potatoes in a saucepan of boiling water and cook for about 10 minutes, depending on the size of the potatoes, until a skewer goes through them easily. Take them out and press the tops lightly with the back of a spoon, to create a 'crack'. Arrange on the prepared tray and put a little bit of butter in each potato. Sprinkle with sea salt and freshly ground black pepper and place a small rosemary sprig on each potato. Bake in the oven for 20 minutes, then reduce the oven tempertaure to 180°C (350°F/Gas 4) to cook the meat — you will leave the potatoes in the oven while the meat cooks.

Meanwhile, prepare the seeded mustard roast beef. Coat the beef on all sides with the seeded mustard. Add to the tray with the potatoes and roast for about 25–30 minutes, depending on how you like the beef cooked. Remove from the oven, wrap the meat in foil and set aside to rest for 10 minutes before serving.

To make the basil tomatoes, finely chop the basil and garlic then transfer to a mortar and use a pestle to pound to a paste with the salt and olive oil. Combine the paste in a bowl with the tomato. Set aside for at least 10 minutes. Just before serving, mix through the balsamic vinegar and season with freshly ground pepper.

Serve slices of beef with a dollop of seeded mustard, a couple of cracked potatoes and some basil tomatoes.

Artwork by
Trent Evans
digital illustration

SEEDED MUSTARD

ROAST BEEF

ROSEMARY

POTATOES

TOMATO

BASIL SALAD

Rooftile semolina gnocchi

One of Rome's classic dishes, 'gnocchi alla romana', resembles the layering of traditional tiled terracotta rooftops in Italy. Serve this gnocchi simply with some freshly grated parmesan, some vegetables or a salad, your favourite pasta topping or a side of meat for a heartier meal.

PREPARATION TIME: 20 MINUTES + 40 MINUTES COOLING
COOKING TIME: 50 MINUTES
SERVES: 4

1 litre (35 fl oz/4 cups) milk
275 g (9¾ oz/1½ cups) semolina
½ teaspoon salt
80 g (2¾ oz) butter, chopped
120 g (4¼ oz/1 cup) finely grated parmesan cheese
2 egg yolks

Lightly grease a flat baking tray, about 30 x 40 cm (12 x 16 inches) or moisten a clean work surface with water.

Heat the milk in a saucepan until nearly boiling, then reduce the heat to low and add the semolina in a steady stream with the salt, whisking constantly. Once combined, use a wooden spoon to stir for 2 minutes, or until thick. Remove from the heat and beat in half of the butter and half of the parmesan cheese, then add the egg yolks, beating with the wooden spoon to prevent them from setting.

Spread the semolina mixture over the greased baking tray or moistened work surface so it is about 1 cm (½ inch) thick. Set aside and allow to cool for about 40 minutes.

Use a 6 cm (2½ inch) round pastry cutter (you can also use a glass or other similar round object) to cut rounds from the semolina, reserving the scraps.

Preheat the oven to 200°C (400°F/Gas 6). Grease a 20 x 30 cm (8 x 12 inch) baking dish. Place the gnocchi in a row along one side of the dish then continue layering it in rows like roof tiles, using the reserved scraps to fill in the edges. Dot with the remaining butter and sprinkle over the remaining parmesan. Bake the gnocchi for about 35–40 minutes, or until it starts to turn golden.

Artwork by
Alexandra Emmons
ink, gouache and watercolour

Sesame-crusted tofu, soba noodle and vegetable stir-fry

Stir-fries are loved for their simplicity, diversity and healthiness, generally packing in a wide variety of vegetables of different textures and colours. The sesame-crusted tofu in this dish adds another level of texture and will have even the toughest of tofu sceptics coming back for seconds.

PREPARATION TIME: 30 MINUTES
COOKING TIME: 20 MINUTES
SERVES: 4

60 ml (2 fl oz/¼ cup) soy sauce,
   plus extra to serve
1 tablespoon oyster sauce
1 tablespoon fish sauce
1 teaspoon caster (superfine) sugar
180 g (6½ oz) soba noodles
1 tablespoon grapeseed oil
1 onion, halved and thinly sliced
3 garlic cloves, thinly sliced
1 tablespoon finely grated ginger
1 bunch broccolini, sliced on the
   diagonal

100 g (3½ oz) snow peas
   (mangetout), trimmed
1 bunch Asian greens (such as
   bok choy/pak choy), trimmed
   and roughly chopped

SESAME-CRUSTED TOFU
grapeseed oil, for frying
500 g (1 lb 2 oz) firm tofu, cut into
   3 cm (1¼ inch) chunks
2 eggs, lightly beaten
200 g (7 oz/1⅓ cups) sesame seeds

In a bowl, mix together the soy sauce, oyster sauce, fish sauce and sugar and set aside.

Bring a saucepan of water to the boil and add the soba noodles. Cook for 3 minutes, then drain and set aside.

To make the sesame-crusted tofu, fill a large heavy-based saucepan with enough grapeseed oil so that it is about 4 cm (1½ inches) deep and place over medium–high heat — the oil is hot enough when a piece of tofu is dropped into the oil and bubbles furiously. Dip the tofu pieces first in the egg, then roll in the sesame seeds to coat. Fry the tofu, in batches, for 1–2 minutes, or until the sesame seeds are golden. Drain on paper towel.

Heat the grapeseed oil in a wok or large heavy-based frying pan over medium–high heat. Add the onion, garlic and ginger and cook for 2–3 minutes. Add the broccolini and stir-fry for 1–2 minutes, then add the snow peas, Asian greens and the soy sauce mixture. Stir-fry for a further 2–3 minutes until the vegetables are just tender but still firm — they will continue to cook after being removed from the heat. Add the soba noodles and toss to combine. Serve with the hot sesame-crusted tofu and extra soy sauce on the side.

Artwork by
Drew Funk
ink on paper

Snail spanakopita

These spinachy spirals equipped us with the highest bargaining power in school lunch trading. Affectionately known as 'spanos' to our family and friends, they are still an almost weekly feature on our dinner tables. Team them with tabouleh (page 154), tomato salsa (page 101) or fattoush (page 90).

PREPARATION TIME: 30 MINUTES
COOKING TIME: 25 MINUTES
MAKES: ABOUT 12

500 g (1 lb 2 oz) frozen spinach, defrosted
  and squeezed of excess moisture
200 g (7 oz/1½ cups) crumbled feta cheese
100 g (3½ oz) ricotta cheese
4 spring onions (scallions), chopped
1 tablespoon finely chopped dill
½ teaspoon freshly grated nutmeg
1 egg, lightly beaten
12–14 sheets filo pastry
50 g (1¾ oz) butter, melted

Heat the oven to 180°C (350°F/Gas 4). Lightly grease a 20 x 30 cm (8 x 12 inch) baking dish. In a bowl, combine the spinach, feta, ricotta, spring onion, dill, nutmeg and egg. Season generously with sea salt and freshly ground black pepper (keeping in mind the feta will be salty) and mix well.

Lay out a sheet of filo on a clean work surface and lightly brush a little butter around the edges. Fold the sheet in half lengthways. Along the longest edge, spread about ¼ cup of spinach mixture in an even line. Fold in the ends and roll gently and tightly into a sausage shape, using the butter to seal the filo. Gently wind the filo into a coil and place in the baking dish. Repeat with the remaining filo and filling, placing them in the dish so they fit snugly.

Brush the tops of the spanakopita with the remaining butter and bake for about 25 minutes, or until the tops are golden. Spanos are as good cold as they are hot.

Artwork by
Pamela Oberman
acrylic on canvas

Fried salt and pepper squid with makeshift aïoli

Squid is an affordable and sustainable seafood option for mealtimes, as well as versatile. You can experiment with a variety of coatings for these fried squid rings — flour, rice flour, breadcrumbs, panko (Japanese breadcrumbs) or semolina combined with different spices, such as Chinese five-spice, chilli flakes, paprika, salt and pepper.

PREPARATION TIME: 20 MINUTES + 1 HOUR FOR FRITES
COOKING TIME: 10 MINUTES
SERVES: 4–6

FRIED SQUID

grapeseed oil, for deep-frying
160 g (5¾ oz/1 cup) rice flour, plain (all-purpose) flour, semolina or panko (Japanese breadcrumbs) or use a combination
2 teaspoons dried chilli flakes
1 teaspoon sea salt
1 teaspoon freshly ground black pepper
4 large squid tubes, sliced into rings about 1 cm (½ inch) wide
frites, to serve (page 58)

MAKESHIFT AÏOLI

85 g (3 oz/⅓ cup) mayonnaise
1½ tablespoons lemon juice
1 tablespoon olive oil
½ teaspoon finely chopped garlic

To make the makeshift aïoli, combine all of the ingredients in a bowl, season with sea salt and freshly ground black pepper and mix well to combine.

To cook the squid, fill a wok or large heavy-based saucepan with enough oil so that it is about 4 cm (1½ inches) deep and place over medium–high heat — the oil should be hot enough so that when a piece of squid is dropped into the oil it bubbles furiously.

Combine the flour, chilli flakes, salt and pepper in a plastic bag. Add the squid rings and shake to coat. Remove the squid from the bag, discarding any excess coating. Deep-fry the squid, in batches, for 2–3 minutes, then remove from the oil with a slotted spoon and drain on paper towel.

Serve the crispy fried squid with plenty of aïoli, fresh salad and frites, or even some soft buns for a squid bap.

Artwork by
Mumptown
digital illustration

Steamed vegetables with miso dressing

This recipe plays homage to a little organic restaurant in NYC, Souen in Soho, which serves nourishing food such as this dish to replenish and restore your soul. You can add a grain such as quinoa or rice to make the meal more substantial.

PREPARATION TIME: 20 MINUTES
COOKING TIME: 20 MINUTES
SERVES: 2

1 kg (2 lb 4 oz) mixed seasonal vegetables
  of your choice, such as pumpkin (winter squash)
  skin left on, cut into large chunks; broccoli florets;
  cauliflower florets; Asian greens, roughly chopped;
  green beans, halved; and carrots, sliced into rounds

MISO DRESSING
60 g (2¼ oz/¼ cup) tahini
60 g (2¼ oz/¼ cup) miso paste

Steam the vegetables in a steamer over a saucepan of boiling water until just tender. Different vegetables will cook at different times, so keep this in mind.

Meanwhile, make the miso dressing. Whisk together the tahini and miso paste in a bowl until smooth. Slowly whisk in just enough water to give a runny consistency.

Pile all of the vegetables onto a serving plate and drizzle over the miso dressing.

Artwork by
Simon MacEwan
watercolour on paper

Who shall have the fishy,

On the little dishy,

Who shall have the salmon,

When the boat comes in.

Tandoori salmon with fragrant rice

The winning combination of rice, fish and greens is undisputed worldwide. Although tandoori paste is available at most supermarkets, it is quick to make and you'll probably have most of the spices in your cupboard.

PREPARATION TIME: 20 MINUTES
COOKING TIME: 20 MINUTES
SERVES: 4

700 g (1 lb 9 oz) boneless salmon fillet
fresh coriander (cilantro) leaves,
    to serve
steamed Asian greens, to serve

TANDOORI PASTE
½ onion, grated
2 garlic cloves, finely chopped
1 small red chilli, seeded and finely
    chopped
2 teaspoons ground coriander
1 teaspoon ground cumin
1 teaspoon paprika
1 teaspoon garam masala
½ teaspoon ground cardamom
a pinch of salt
60 ml (2 fl oz/¼ cup) lemon juice
190 g (6¾ oz/⅔ cup) plain yoghurt

FRAGRANT RICE
1 tablespoon grapeseed oil
1 small onion, thinly sliced into rings
1 garlic clove, crushed
2 cm (¾ inch) piece fresh ginger
6 cardamom pods, bruised
6 whole cloves
1 star anise
3 cm (1¼ inch) strip lemon rind,
    white pith removed
150 g (5½ oz/¾ cup) basmati rice
125 ml (4 fl oz/½ cup) chicken stock

To make the tandoori paste, use a mortar and pestle to pound together the onion, garlic and chilli to make a paste. Alternatively, you can use a small food processor. Add the spices, salt and lemon juice and mix well. Combine 3 tablespoons of the tandoori mixture with the yoghurt and stir to combine.

Heat the oven to 180°C (350°F/Gas 4) and lightly grease a baking tray. Coat the salmon in the tandoori mixture and place on the prepared tray. Bake for about 15 minutes, or until the fish is cooked but still slightly pink in the middle — the fish will continue to cook after you remove it from the oven.

Meanwhile, make the fragrant rice. Heat the grapeseed oil in a saucepan over medium heat. Add the onion and garlic and cook for 2–3 minutes, or until softened. Add the ginger, cardamom pods, cloves and star anise and cook for a further 1–2 minutes, then add the lemon rind, rice, stock and 185 ml (6 fl oz/¾ cup) water. Stir well and bring to the boil, reduce the heat to the lowest setting possible, cover, and simmer for 15 minutes. Remove the pan from the heat but do not remove the lid, and set aside to steam for a further 5 minutes, then fluff the rice with a fork.

Divide the salmon between plates with the fragrant rice and serve with some steamed Asian greens on the side.

Artwork by
Jennifer Hillhouse
watercolour and digital illustration

Sushi platter

Making sushi is great for entertaining as it is fun to prepare and made much easier by getting a group involved. It is also a good option for gatherings where you need to cater for people's preferences and dietary requirements. Once you've made the sushi rice, the choice of fillings is completely up to you. Keep cut vegetables such as carrot and cucumber in a bowl of iced water to keep them fresh. You will need at least one bamboo sushi mat for rolling, but having a few on hand will make light work.

PREPARATION TIME: 30 MINUTES
COOKING TIME: 30 MINUTES
SERVES: 4

nori sheets (dried seaweed)

SUSHI RICE

440 g (15½ oz/2 cups) sushi rice or short-grain rice
60 ml (2 fl oz/¼ cup) rice wine vinegar
2 tablespoons caster (superfine) sugar

TUNA SALAD FILLING

200 g (7 oz) tin tuna, drained
2 tablespoons mayonnaise
1 spring onion (scallion), finely chopped
1 teaspoon soy sauce

MARINATED TOFU FILLING

2 tablespoons mirin
60 ml (2 fl oz/¼ cup) soy sauce
½ teaspoon sesame oil
200 g (7 oz) firm tofu, cut into long thin strips
1 tablespoon grapeseed oil

TAMAGOYAKI (ROLLED OMELETTE) FILLING

4 eggs
1 teaspoon dashi powder mixed with 60 ml (2 fl oz/¼ cup) water
1½ tablespoons caster (superfine) sugar
2 teaspoons soy sauce
2 teaspoons mirin
1 tablespoon grapeseed oil

ADDITIONAL FILLINGS

2 avocados, peeled, stones removed and cut into long thin strips
150 g (5½ oz) fresh salmon, sliced into thin strips
150 g (5½ oz) fresh tuna, sliced into thin strips
cucumber, cut in half lengthways, then into long thin slices
carrot, peeled, cut in half lengthways, then into long thin slices
iceberg lettuce, shredded
pickled ginger, to serve
wasabi, to serve
soy sauce, to serve
Japanese mayonnaise, to serve
sesame seeds, to serve

To make the sushi rice, rinse the rice thoroughly and drain well. Place in a saucepan with 625 ml (21½ fl oz/2½ cups) water and bring to the boil, then reduce the heat to low, cover, and simmer for 15 minutes. Remove from the heat and allow to stand, covered, for a further 10 minutes. Allow to cool completely.

CONTINUED →

Artwork by
Warren Handley
digital collage

In a small saucepan, combine the vinegar and sugar and stir over medium heat until the sugar has dissolved. Remove from the heat and allow to cool (this is called 'sushi-zu' or sushi vinegar).

Add the *sushi-zu* to the cooled rice and use a wooden spoon to gently combine, making sure the vinegar is evenly distributed.

To make the tuna salad, combine all of the ingredients in a bowl. Refrigerate until ready to roll.

To make the marinated tofu, combine the mirin, soy sauce and sesame oil in a bowl, add the tofu and leave to marinate for at least 15 minutes. Heat the grapeseed oil in a small frying pan over medium–high heat and cook the tofu for 5 minutes, turning occasionally. Remove from the pan and allow to cool.

To make the *tamagoyaki*, whisk together the eggs, dashi, sugar, soy sauce and mirin in a bowl. Heat the grapeseed oil in the same pan, then add the egg mixture and cook until the omelette has set most of the way through, then flip and cook the other side. Remove the egg from the pan and cut into 1 cm (½ inch) strips.

To assemble the sushi, place one nori sheet, shiny side down, on a bamboo mat — make sure the longest edge is at the top of the mat. Dip your hands in water to prevent the rice from sticking to them while you work. Grab a small handful of rice and spread over the bottom two-thirds of the nori sheet. Arrange your preferred fillings in a horizontal strip in the middle of the rice. Begin to roll the sushi mat from the end closest to you, tucking your fingers underneath as you roll to ensure no ingredients spill out. Seal the nori with a dab of water. Cut the roll into 2 cm (¾ inch) slices using a sharp knife dipped in water, cleaning the blade as soon as the rice starts to stick.

Serve the sushi with pickled ginger, wasabi, soy sauce and Japanese mayonnaise.

Parmesan-crusted lamb chops with potato bake and a red cabbage and broad bean salad

These classic Italian-style lamb chops are dressed up in a crunchy golden coat of parmesan and breadcrumbs that will have you picking them up with both hands to devour them. The red cabbage and broad bean salad brings vibrancy and freshness to the plate, matched with a no-fuss potato bake for a well-rounded plate.

PREPARATION TIME: 30 MINUTES
COOKING TIME: 50 MINUTES
SERVES: 4

POTATO BAKE
1 kg (2 lb 4 oz) all-purpose potatoes, such as desiree, scrubbed and very thinly sliced
80 ml (2½ fl oz/⅓ cup) olive oil

RED CABBAGE AND BROAD BEAN SALAD
½ red cabbage, thinly sliced (use green if unavailable)
400 g (14 oz/2 cups) frozen broad (fava) beans
10 g (¼ oz/½ cup) mint, chopped
10 g (¼ oz/½ cup) flat-leaf (Italian) parsley, chopped

125 ml (4 fl oz/½ cup) red wine vinegar
60 ml (2 fl oz/¼ cup) olive oil
1 teaspoon sugar
1 teaspoon salt

PARMESAN-CRUSTED LAMB CHOPS
2 eggs
100 g (3½ oz/¾ cup) finely grated parmesan cheese
40 g (1½ oz/⅓ cup) fresh breadcrumbs (or use dry if unavailable)
olive oil, for cooking
8 lamb chops

To make the potato bake, preheat the oven to 180°C (350°F/Gas 4). Grease a 20 x 30 cm (8 x 12 inch) baking dish with some olive oil. Wash the potato slices in cold water and pat them dry with paper towel (this will remove any excess starch). Arrange the potato slices in the dish in layers, sprinkling with a little oil, sea salt and freshly ground black pepper between each, then drizzle with the remaining oil and bake in the oven for 40 minutes, or until golden.

Meanwhile, make the red cabbage and broad bean salad. Steam the cabbage in a steamer placed over a saucepan of boiling water until just cooked, then refresh immediately in cold water to prevent further cooking; drain well. Cook the broad beans in a saucepan of boiling water for 2–3 minutes, or until just tender. Drain, and when cool enough to handle, peel and discard the skins. Combine the cooked cabbage, broad beans, mint and parsley in a bowl. In a separate bowl, mix together the red wine vinegar, olive oil, sugar and salt. Stir through the salad.

CONTINUED →→

To make the parmesan-crusted lamb chops, beat the eggs in a large shallow dish. In a separate dish, combine the parmesan and breadcrumbs. Flatten the chops slightly with a meat tenderiser, or use the end of a rolling pin or a pestle.

Pour enough oil into a heavy-based frying pan to reach a depth of 1 cm (½ inch) and place over medium heat. Dip both sides of the chops first into the beaten egg, then in the parmesan crumbs. When the oil is hot, add the chops and cook over medium–low heat for 2–3 minutes on each side, or until cooked and golden.

Serve the chops with a large helping of potato bake and the cabbage and broad bean salad.

Artwork by
Billie Justice Thomson
acrylic on perspex

White fish donburi

This is like the Japanese equivalent of a big comforting bowl of pasta. A donburi is a bowl of hot steamed rice that can be topped with a variety of ingredients. This donburi features rare, thinly sliced fish marinated in Japanese seasonings, with a flavoursome topping of fresh herbs and sesame sauce.

PREPARATION TIME: 20 MINUTES + 40 MINUTES MARINATING
COOKING TIME: 5 MINUTES
SERVES: 4

80 ml (2½ fl oz/⅓ cup) mirin
80 ml (2½ fl oz/⅓ cup) sake
60 ml (2 fl oz/¼ cup) soy sauce
1 teaspoon finely grated ginger
500 g (1 lb 2 oz) skinless, boneless firm white fish fillets, such as mahi mahi
1 tablespoon grapeseed oil
1 quantity sushi rice (pages 130–32)
2 tablespoons finely grated daikon
2 tablespoons shredded nori (dried seaweed)
2 tablespoons chopped mint
2 tablespoons chopped basil
2 tablespoons chopped flat-leaf (Italian) parsley
2 spring onions (scallions), very thinly sliced
1 tablespoon sesame seeds, lightly toasted

SESAME DRESSING
2 tablespoons tahini
1 tablespoon caster (superfine) sugar
¼ teaspoon dashi powder mixed with 1 tablespoon water (see note page 132)
1 tablespoon mirin
1 tablespoon soy sauce

To make the sesame dressing, whisk together all of the ingredients in a small bowl. Set aside.

Combine the mirin, sake, soy sauce and ginger in a shallow dish large enough to hold the fish. Add the fish and marinate for 20 minutes on each side.

Heat the grapeseed oil in a large frying pan over high heat. Add the fish and sear on both sides until it is cooked on the outside but not in the middle — this will take about 2 minutes on each side for a 3 cm (1¼ inch) thick fillet. Remove the fish from the pan and leave to rest for 1 minute, then slice thinly.

To serve, divide the rice between serving bowls. Lay the fish slices over the top and scatter with the daikon, nori, herbs, spring onion, sesame seeds and sesame dressing, to taste.

Artwork by
Daniel O'Toole
ink and watercolour on paper

Vietnamese-style squid salad

This dish has all the sharp, tangy and refreshing flavours characteristic of Vietnamese food, such as lemongrass, chilli, coriander and fish sauce. The squid marinade also works with other ingredients, such as prawns, pork, octopus or chicken.

PREPARATION TIME: 30 MINUTES + 30 MINUTES MARINATING
COOKING TIME: 10 MINUTES
SERVES: 4

VIETNAMESE SQUID

- 4 squid tubes
- 2 cm (¾ inch) piece lemongrass, white part only, finely chopped
- 4 garlic cloves, peeled
- 2 teaspoons finely grated ginger
- 1½ tablespoons fish sauce
- 1½ tablespoons soy sauce
- 1 teaspoon sesame oil
- 1 teaspoon grapeseed oil, plus extra for frying
- 1 tablespoon palm sugar (jaggery) or soft brown sugar
- 1 teaspoon Chinese five-spice powder

VIETNAMESE SALAD

- 100 g (3½ oz) rice noodles, cooked and cooled
- ½ iceberg lettuce, shredded
- 1 red capsicum (pepper), seeded and thinly sliced
- 1 Lebanese (short) cucumber, halved lengthways and sliced
- 50 g (1¾ oz/⅓ cup) roasted salted peanuts, roughly chopped
- ½ red onion, very thinly sliced
- 25 g (1 oz/½ cup) chopped coriander (cilantro) leaves
- 15 g (½ oz/¼ cup) chopped mint
- 15 g (½ oz/¼ cup) chopped basil
- 1 long red chilli, seeded and finely chopped
- 2 tablespoons fish sauce
- 80 ml (2½ fl oz/⅓ cup) lime juice
- 1 tablespoon palm sugar (jaggery) or soft brown sugar

Cut the squid tubes in half lengthways, then rinse well and pat dry. Score the inside of the squid in a crisscross pattern, without cutting through it, then cut the squid into rough trapezium shapes. Use a food processor or a mortar and pestle to process or pound together the lemongrass, garlic and ginger. Add the fish sauce, soy sauce, sesame and grapeseed oils, palm sugar and five-spice and mix to combine. Add the squid to the marinade, toss to coat, and set aside for 30 minutes.

Meanwhile, make the Vietnamese salad. Combine the rice noodles, lettuce, capsicum, cucumber, peanuts, onion, coriander, mint and basil in a large bowl. In a separate bowl, mix together the chilli, fish sauce, lime juice and palm sugar. Toss the dressing through the salad to coat.

Heat a wok or large frying pan with a little oil. When the oil is very hot add the squid — it will curl and turn white when cooked, usually about 3 minutes. Be careful not to overcook it as this will make it tough. Serve the squid hot off the wok and the salad chilled or at room temperature.

Artwork by
Hilde Thomsen
ink and watercolour on paper

Zucchini fritters

Well-balanced in flavour and form, these fritters are crisp and golden on the outside, gooey on the inside, cheesy and minty fresh. They make for a great midweek dinner or weekend lunch option. Team them with your favourite salad or salsa, or top them with a poached egg for breakfast.

PREPARATION TIME: 20 MINUTES +10 MINUTES SALTING
COOKING TIME: 20 MINUTES
MAKES: 12 FRITTERS

450 g (1 lb/3⅓ cups) grated zucchini (courgette)
1 teaspoon salt
150 g (5½ oz) feta cheese, crumbled
15 g (½ oz/¼ cup) mint, finely chopped
10 g (¼ oz/⅓ cup) flat-leaf (Italian) parsley, finely chopped
3 spring onions (scallions), finely chopped
   (or use ½ onion, grated)
75 g (2¾ oz/½ cup) plain (all-purpose) flour
1 egg, lightly beaten
olive oil, for frying

Place the zucchini in a colander, sprinkle with salt and leave for 10 minutes to bring out the moisture.

Use your hands to squeeze as much liquid from the zucchini as possible. Place in a mixing bowl with the feta, mint, parsley and spring onion and season with sea salt and freshly ground black pepper. Mix everything together, stir through the flour, then add the egg and stir to combine.

Heat the olive oil in a frying pan over medium heat — the oil should be about 1 cm (½ inch) deep. When the oil is hot, drop ⅓ cup of the zucchini mixture into the pan at a time and flatten into a patty shape — you may need cook them in batches. Cook the fritters for 2–3 minutes to cook well on one side before flipping to cook for a further 2–3 minutes, or until golden on both sides. Drain on paper towel and repeat until all are cooked.

Serve the zucchini fritters hot with some tomato salsa (page 101), tabouleh (page 154) or a dollop of sweet chilli sauce on the side.

Artwork by
King Adz
mixed media

Vegetables on the side

Adding new vegetable dishes to your repertoire is always a good thing, so here are a few of our favourites.

PREPARATION TIME: EACH TYPE TAKES ABOUT 15 MINUTES
COOKING TIME: VARIED
SERVES: 4 AS A SIDE

Roasted amaretto pumpkin

400 g (14 oz) pumpkin (winter squash),
    skin left one, seeds removed, and flesh chopped
    into 2 cm (¾ inch) pieces
2 tablespoons olive oil
4 amaretto biscuits (these are available at delis and
    some supermarkets, but you can substitute for
    another strongly scented almond biscuit)

Preheat the oven to 180°C (350°F/Gas 4). Arrange the pumpkin on a baking tray, drizzle with the olive oil, season with sea salt and freshly ground black pepper then toss to combine. Crumble the amaretto biscuits over the pumpkin and bake in the oven for 15 minutes, or until the pumpkin is just soft. Remove from the oven and serve immediately.

Fennel roasted in parmesan and breadcrumbs

2 fennel bulbs
2 tablespoons olive oil
100 g (3½ oz/¾ cup) finely grated parmesan cheese
110 g (3¾ oz/1 cup) dry breadcrumbs

Preheat the oven to 180°C (350°F/Gas 4). Cut each fennel bulb in half and remove and discard the core. Slice along the grain into wedges, about 2 cm (¾ inch) thick. Arrange the fennel on a baking tray, drizzle with half of the olive oil and toss well.

In a separate bowl, mix together the parmesan, breadcrumbs and remaining oil and season with sea salt and freshly ground black pepper. Sprinkle the parmesan crumb mixture over the fennel and bake in the oven for 30–40 minutes, or until the fennel is golden and tender. Remove from the oven and serve immediately.

Artwork by
Liam Stevens
cut paper

Spiced fried cauliflower

2 tablespoons grapeseed oil
½ teaspoon ground cumin
½ teaspoon ground coriander
½ teaspoon sweet paprika
½ teaspoon cayenne pepper
½ teaspoon ground cinnamon
½ teaspoon salt
500 g (1 lb 2 oz/4 cups) cauliflower florets

Heat the grapeseed oil in a large frying pan or wok over medium heat. Add all of the spices and cook until fragrant, about 1 minute. Add the cauliflower and toss well to coat in the spices. Cover and continue to cook over medium–low heat for about 10–15 minutes, or until the cauliflower has softened.

Sautéed brussels sprouts

300 g (10½ oz) brussels sprouts
40 g (1½ oz) unsalted butter
½ teaspoon freshly grated nutmeg

Place the brussels sprouts in a saucepan and pour in enough water to cover. Bring to the boil, then reduce the heat to low and simmer for 15–20 minutes, or until just tender. Drain and set aside to cool for 5 minutes, then slice each brussels sprout in half lengthways.

Heat the butter in a frying pan over medium–low heat, add the nutmeg and stir for 1–2 minutes, or until fragrant. Add the brussels sprouts, increase the heat and cook for 5 minutes on each side, or until they start to brown and become crisp. Season the brussels sprouts with sea salt and freshly ground black pepper, to taste, before serving.

Cabbage, poppyseed and walnut fry

1 tablespoon olive oil
2 teaspoons black poppy seeds
250 g (9 oz/2 cups) roughly chopped walnuts
½ white cabbage, thinly sliced
1 tablespoon lemon juice

Heat the oil in a large saucepan over medium–high heat. Add the poppy seeds and cook until they start to pop. Add the walnuts and cook until they start to turn golden, then add the cabbage and stir-fry until the cabbage is just softened. Drizzle with the lemon juice, season with sea salt and freshly ground black pepper and serve immediately.

Roasted broccoli with chilli and lemon

1 large broccoli head, stems removed and broken into florets
60 ml (2 fl oz/¼ cup) olive oil
1 teaspoon dried chilli flakes
finely grated zest of 1 large lemon
juice of 1 large lemon

Preheat the oven to 180°C (350°F/Gas 4). In a large bowl, combine the broccoli, olive oil, chilli flakes and lemon zest and toss until well combined. Transfer to a baking tray and roast in the oven for 7–8 minutes, or until the broccoli starts to brown. Turn and roast for another 3–4 minutes. Remove the broccoli from the oven, season with sea salt and freshly ground black pepper and squeeze the lemon juice over the warm broccoli (doing this when it's warm helps it to absorb the citrus juice). Serve immediately.

Kale with onion and chickpeas

2 tablespoons olive oil
1 onion, thinly sliced
1 bunch kale, roughly chopped
310 g (11 oz) tin chickpeas, rinsed and drained

Heat the olive oil in a frying pan over medium–high heat. Add the onion and cook for 5–7 minutes, or until the onion begins to brown. Add the kale and chickpeas and cook for a further 3–4 minutes, or until the kale softens. Season with sea salt and freshly ground black pepper and serve immediately.

Banquets

From how you lay the table, to who prepares the meal, your accompanying drink, the utensils you use and what you say to start the meal, rituals for banquets vary greatly around the world. In this chapter you'll find a selection of colourful banquets from a mixture of cuisines. Each menu is designed to feed six or more people, and features additional dishes that can be included when your dinner-guest numbers creep up, or if you're planning a packed lunch for the next day. Elements of these meals can be cooked individually or together, depending on the occasion and your appetite.

Japanese banquet

This classy banquet is made up of dishes that are typical of the refined flavours of Japanese fare. Although the ingredients sound exotic, most can be found in your local supermarket. The unusually sour umeboshi (pickled plums) are sold at most Asian grocery stores. We recommend accompanying the banquet with some rice, extra soy sauce, pickled ginger and wasabi.

PREPARATION TIME: 30 MINUTES + 30 MINUTES MARINATING
COOKING TIME: 20 MINUTES
SERVES: 8

Marinated steak with herb and dashi topping

185 ml (6 fl oz/¾ cup) soy sauce
185 ml (6 fl oz/¾ cup) mirin
185 ml (6 fl oz/¾ cup) sake
2 teaspoons finely grated ginger, plus 1 teaspoon extra to serve
750 g (1 lb 10 oz) sirloin steak, sliced into 3 mm (⅛ inch) thick strips
1 tablespoon grapeseed oil
3 spring onions (scallions), finely chopped, to serve
15 g (½ oz/¼ cup) finely chopped mint, to serve
15 g (½ oz/¼ cup) roughly chopped basil, to serve

DASHI TOPPING
3 g (¹⁄₁₆ oz) packet dashi powder mixed
   with 185 ml (6 fl oz/¾ cup) water (see note page 132)
80 ml (2½ fl oz/⅓ cup) soy sauce
80 ml (2½ fl oz/⅓ cup) mirin
1 teaspoon sugar

Combine the soy sauce, mirin, sake and ginger in a large bowl. Add the beef and mix well to coat. Set aside to marinate for at least 30 minutes.

Meanwhile, to make the dashi topping, put the dashi, soy sauce, mirin and sugar in a saucepan over medium–high heat. Bring to the boil, then reduce the heat to low and simmer for 5 minutes. Remove from the heat.

Heat the grapeseed oil in a wok or large frying pan over medium–high heat. Remove the steak from the marinade and discard the marinade. Cook the beef, in batches, for 30–60 seconds on each side, or until the meat is cooked to medium–rare. Remove from the wok and arrange on a serving dish.

To serve, combine the spring onion, mint, basil and extra grated ginger in a bowl and mix well. Pour the dashi topping over the beef and scatter the herb mixture over the top.

Daikon salad with umeboshi dressing

500 g (1 lb 2 oz) daikon
4 Japanese pickled plums (umeboshi), seeds removed and flesh mashed
60 ml (2 fl oz/¼ cup) rice wine vinegar
1 tablespoon caster (superfine) sugar
1 tablespoon olive oil

Grate the daikon about 30 minutes before you are ready to make the salad and sit it in a colander over a bowl to drain off any excess liquid.

Place the pickled plums, vinegar, sugar and olive oil in a food processor and blend to make a smooth paste. Transfer to a small saucepan over medium heat and stir until the sugar has dissolved, then remove from the heat and allow to cool.

Spread the grated daikon out in a serving plate and top with the umeboshi mixture. Refrigerate until ready to serve.

Miso eggplant

2 tablespoons miso paste
2 tablespoons sake or dry white wine
2 tablespoons mirin
1 tablespoon soy sauce
1 tablespoon caster (superfine) sugar
60 ml (2 fl oz/¼ cup) grapeseed oil
1 large eggplant (aubergine), sliced into
   1 cm (½ inch) rounds, then into smaller wedges
2 spring onions (scallions), thinly sliced

In a small saucepan over low heat, whisk together the miso, sake, mirin, soy sauce, sugar and 2 tablespoons hot water. Stir for 1–2 minutes, or until the sugar has completely dissolved.

Heat the grapeseed oil in a wok or large frying pan over medium–high heat. Add the eggplant and cook for about 5 minutes, or until slightly softened. Add the miso mixture and spring onion and cook for a further 5 minutes, or until the eggplant has softened a little more and the sauce has thickened. Remove from the heat, transfer to a serving plate and serve immediately.

Green beans with sesame dressing

1 tablespoon sesame seeds
⅛ teaspoon dashi powder mixed with 1 tablespoon water
  (see note page 132)
1 tablespoon soy sauce
1 tablespoon tahini
2 teaspoons caster (superfine) sugar
350 g (12 oz) fresh green beans, trimmed

Use a mortar and pestle to finely grind the sesame seeds, then transfer to a bowl and combine with the dashi mixture, soy sauce, tahini and sugar.

Steam or boil the green beans until just tender, then immediately refresh in cold water to stop the cooking process. Arrange the beans on a serving plate and top with the sesame dressing.

Cucumber salad

1 telegraph (long) cucumber
60 ml (2 fl oz/¼ cup) rice wine vinegar
2 teaspoons caster (superfine) sugar

Cut the cucumber in half lengthways, then thinly slice on the diagonal. Place in a bowl.

In a separate bowl, mix together the vinegar and sugar, stirring until the sugar has dissolved. Add to the cucumber and toss well. Refrigerate until ready to serve.

Middle Eastern banquet

What's not to love about sweet and sour tabouleh, crispy, nutty falafel and juicy lamb smothered in an array of sauces? This banquet has always been the last meal we request before we go away, and the first when we come home. Serve this banquet with a yoghurt tahini sauce (equal parts yoghurt and tahini mixed together with a little salt), plain yoghurt and sweet chilli sauce.

PREPARATION TIME: 40 MINUTES + 35 MINUTES SOAKING FOR BURGHUL
+ 1 HOUR 35 MINUTES RISING FOR PITTA BREAD
COOKING TIME: 35 MINUTES
SERVES: 8

Falafels
MAKES 20-24

45 g (1½ oz/¼ cup) burghul (bulgur)
2 x 400 g (14 oz) tins chickpeas, rinsed and drained
½ onion, grated and squeezed of excess moisture
1 garlic clove, chopped
15 g (½ oz/½ cup) roughly chopped flat-leaf (Italian) parsley
15 g (½ oz/¼ cup) roughly chopped coriander (cilantro) leaves
2 tablespoons roughly chopped mint
2 teaspoons ground cumin
2 teaspoons ground coriander
½ teaspoon baking powder
1 teaspoon salt
1 teaspoon freshly ground black pepper
2 tablespoons plain (all-purpose) flour
olive oil, for frying

Put the burghul in a bowl, cover with hot water and leave to soak for 15 minutes to soften. Drain and squeeze out any excess liquid.

Combine the chickpeas, onion, garlic, parsley, coriander and mint in a food processor and process until roughly chopped. Add the burghul and all of the remaining ingredients, except the olive oil, and blend until just combined. Remove half of the mixture and set aside in a bowl. Blend the rest until almost smooth. Combine with the reserved half, using a spoon, to make textured falafels.

Pour enough olive oil into a large frying pan so it is about 1 cm (½ inch) deep and place over medium–high heat. When the oil is hot, cook the falafels for 2–3 minutes on each side, or until golden. Drain on paper towel and serve hot.

Artwork by
Rachel Bartram
mixed media

Lamb skewers

500 g (1 lb 2 oz) minced (ground) lamb
2 spring onions (scallions) or 1 small onion, finely chopped
4 garlic cloves, finely chopped
2 tablespoons tomato paste (concentrated purée)
1 teaspoon finely grated lemon zest
1 tablespoon lemon juice
15 g (1 oz/½ cup) finely chopped flat-leaf (Italian) parsley
15 g (1 oz/¼ cup) finely chopped coriander (cilantro) leaves
½ teaspoon ground cinnamon
40 g (1½ oz/¼ cup) pine nuts, toasted (optional)
1 egg, beaten
olive oil, for frying

Soak 12 bamboo skewers in water for 10 minutes to prevent them from burning during cooking. Combine all of the ingredients, except for the olive oil, in a large bowl and use your hands to mix everything together. Take a small handful of the mixture and shape into a small sausage around a skewer. Repeat with the remaining mixture.

Lightly grease a large frying pan or barbecue hotplate with the olive oil. Cook the lamb skewers over medium–high heat for 2–3 minutes on each side, or until golden brown and cooked through. Serve hot.

Tabouleh

130 g (4¾ oz/¾ cup) burghul (bulgur)
6 spring onions (scallions), finely chopped
120 g (4¼ oz/4 cups) finely chopped curly parsley
15 g (½ oz/¼ cup) finely chopped mint
4 large tomatoes, finely diced
60 ml (2 fl oz/¼ cup) olive oil
60 ml (2 fl oz/¼ cup) lemon juice

Place the burghul and spring onion in a bowl and pour over enough hot water to cover. Allow to stand for about 20 minutes. Drain and press out any excess liquid. Combine the burghul mixture in a bowl with the parsley, mint and tomato.

In a separate bowl, combine the olive oil and lemon juice and season with sea salt and freshly ground black pepper. Add to the bowl with the burghul and toss to combine. Refrigerate until ready to serve.

Watermelon and feta salad

3 cups seedless watermelon, cut into small chunks
100 g (3½ oz) feta cheese, cut into cubes
75 g (2¾ oz/½ cup) pitted kalamata olives
15 g (½ oz/¼ cup) torn mint leaves
2 tablespoons olive oil (a fruity variety works well in this salad)
1 tablespoon balsamic vinegar

Combine the watermelon, feta, olives and mint in a serving bowl. Drizzle over the olive oil and balsamic vinegar and toss gently to coat. Refrigerate until ready to serve.

Pitta bread

300 g (10½ oz/2 cups) plain (all-purpose) flour
150 g (5½ oz/1 cup) wholemeal (whole-wheat) flour
1 tablespoon caster (superfine) sugar
7 g (¼ oz/2 teaspoons) active dried yeast
1 teaspoon salt
2 tablespoons olive oil, plus extra for the bowl

Combine the plain and wholemeal flours in a large bowl with the sugar, yeast and salt. Add the olive oil and 250 ml (9 fl oz/1 cup) water and mix until it comes together to form a dough. If the mixture is too dry, add a little more water — if the mixture is too sticky, add a little more flour. Shape into a ball, then turn out onto a lightly floured work surface and knead for 10 minutes. Alternatively, use an electric mixer fitted with a dough hook attachment and process for about 4 minutes. The goal is a very smooth and elastic dough.

Place the dough in a bowl coated lightly with oil, cover with a clean damp tea towel (dish towel) and set aside in a warm place to rise for 1 hour, or until doubled in size.

Punch the dough down and divide into 10 evenly-sized portions. Roll each portion into a ball, place on a lightly floured work surface, cover with a damp tea towel again, and leave to rise for a further 20 minutes.

Preheat the oven to 200°C (400°F/Gas 6) and lightly grease two large baking trays. Roll each ball into a flat circle with a 15 cm (6 inch) diameter. Place the pitta circles on the prepared trays and set aside to rise for 15 minutes. Working in batches, bake the pitta breads in the oven for about 10 minutes, or until they start to brown. Keep warm while cooking the remainder.

Indian banquet

Indian food excites people with its full spectrum of flavours, bound together by an extensive array of chutneys, pickles, salads, raitas and flat breads. The chutneys on pages 47–48 would go well with this banquet. You could also serve up a traditional beverage such as some spiced black tea or a mango lassi, made by blending mango, yoghurt, milk, sugar and a pinch of ground cardamom.

PREPARATION TIME: 45 MINUTES
COOKING TIME: 2 HOURS
SERVES: 8

Rogan josh

80 g (2¾ oz) ghee or 80 ml (2½ fl oz/⅓ cup) grapeseed oil
8 cardamom pods, bruised
2 teaspoons whole cloves
1 teaspoon fennel seeds
2 onions, chopped
3 garlic cloves, finely chopped
1 tablespoon finely grated ginger
2 teaspoons ground coriander
2 teaspoons ground cumin
1 teaspoon chilli powder
1 teaspoon ground turmeric
1 teaspoon salt
130 g (4¾ oz/½ cup) plain yoghurt
400g (14 oz) tin whole tomatoes, roughly chopped
1 kg (2 lb 4 oz) lamb, cut into 2 cm (¾ inch) pieces
140 g (5 oz/1 cup) frozen or fresh peas
1 teaspoon garam masala
35 g (1¼ oz/¼ cup) slivered almonds, roasted
25 g (1 oz/½ cup) chopped coriander (cilantro) leaves

Heat the ghee or grapeseed oil in a large saucepan over medium–high heat. Add the cardamom pods, cloves and fennel seeds and cook for 1 minute, or until fragrant. Add the onion, garlic and ginger and cook for about 5 minutes, or until the onion has softened. Add the remaining spices and salt and cook for a further 3–4 minutes. Stir in the yoghurt, add the tomatoes and simmer for 5 minutes.

Add the lamb to the pan and stir to coat, then cover and cook over low heat, stirring occasionally for 1–1½ hours, or until the lamb is very tender. Add the peas and cook for 5 minutes, or until the peas are tender, then stir through the garam masala. Transfer to a serving bowl and sprinkle over the roasted almonds and coriander before serving.

Artwork by
Clay Hickson
pencil on paper

Eggplant pickle

125 ml (4 fl oz/½ cup) grapeseed oil
6 garlic cloves, chopped
2 tablespoons finely grated ginger
1 teaspoon ground cumin
1 teaspoon fenugreek seeds
1 teaspoon chilli powder
1 teaspoon ground turmeric
500 g (1 lb 2 oz) eggplant (aubergine), cut into small cubes
60 ml (2 fl oz/¼ cup) cider vinegar
1 tablespoon soft brown sugar
2 teaspoons salt

Heat the grapeseed oil in a saucepan over medium–high heat. Add the garlic and ginger and cook for about 2 minutes, or until softened. Add the cumin, fenugreek seeds, chilli powder and turmeric and cook for 1–2 minutes, or until fragrant. Add the eggplant, vinegar, sugar and salt and stir well, then cover and simmer for about 30 minutes, stirring occasionally, until the eggplant has broken down. Remove from the heat and allow to cool before serving.

Dhal

2 tablespoons ghee or grapeseed oil
1 onion, thinly sliced into rings
1 tablespoon finely grated ginger
1 teaspoon ground cumin
1 teaspoon ground turmeric
1 teaspoon chilli powder
1 teaspoon ground cinnamon
205 g (7¼ oz/1 cup) red lentils, rinsed and drained
1 teaspoon lemon juice
2 teaspoons salt

Heat the ghee or grapeseed oil in a saucepan over medium–high heat. Add the onion and ginger and cook for 2–3 minutes, then add the spices and cook for a further 1–2 minutes, or until fragrant — if the mixture becomes too dry at any stage add a dash more oil or water.

Add the lentils and mix well, then pour in 500 ml (17 fl oz/2 cups) water and the salt and bring to the boil. Reduce the heat to low and simmer, uncovered, for about 15–20 minutes, or until the lentils are soft and the dhal has thickened. Remove from the heat, stir through the lemon juice and serve hot.

Tomato mint salad

3 large tomatoes
½ onion, finely diced
15 g (½ oz/¼ cup) finely chopped mint
a pinch of salt

Cut the tops off the tomatoes and squeeze out the seeds. Finely dice them and place in a bowl with the onion, mint and salt and toss to combine.

Cucumber raita

1 Lebanese (short) cucumber
a pinch of salt
260 g (9¼ oz/1 cup) plain yoghurt
½ garlic clove, crushed
½ teaspoon sweet paprika
squeeze of lemon, to taste

Cut the cucumber in half lengthways, scoop out and discard the seeds and grate the flesh. Place in a colander and sprinkle with salt. Set aside for 20 minutes.

Use your hands to squeeze and press out the excess moisture from the cucumber, then add to a bowl with the yoghurt, garlic and paprika. Adjust the flavour with lemon juice and salt, to taste. Refrigerate until ready to serve.

Mango raita

1 small mango, peeled, stone removed and flesh chopped
130 g (4¾ oz/½ cup) plain yoghurt
½ garlic clove, finely chopped
a pinch of salt

Put the mango, yoghurt and garlic in a blender or food processor and blend to combine. Add salt, to taste.

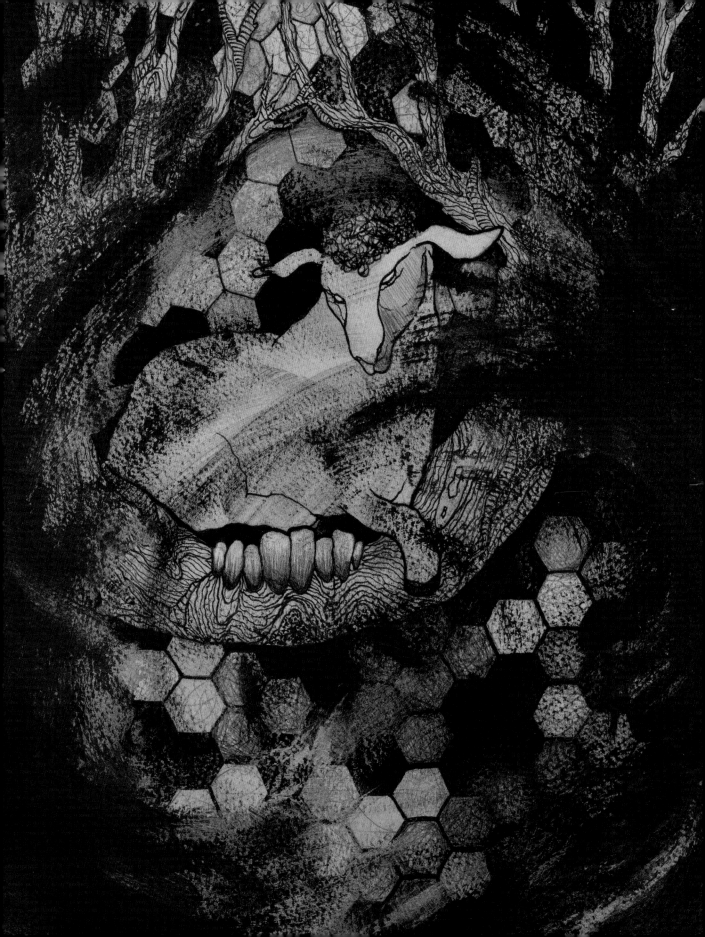

Moroccan banquet

Tagines get their name from the traditional earthenware pot in which they are cooked. The distinct conical lid traps in moisture for the long cooking time, to evenly cook the contents and produce succulent and flavoursome one-pot combinations of meats, vegetables, fruits, nuts and spices. If you don't have a tagine you can use a casserole dish or large heavy-based saucepan with a lid.

For this banquet, we've provided different variations for a tagine — a lamb, a chicken and a vegetable — all of which pair well with the fragrant little side salads. Tagines are also traditionally served with steaming mounds of buttery couscous (page 105). If you're looking for a traditional beverage to accompany this banquet, Moroccan mint tea is a cultural staple — combine piping hot brewed green tea with fresh stems of mint leaves and sugar.

PREPARATION TIME: 40 MINUTES + 30 MINUTES MARINATING THE CHICKEN
COOKING TIME: 1 HOUR 45 MINUTES
SERVES: 8

Lamb and prune tagine

200 g (7 oz/1 cup) pitted prunes
2 tablespoons olive oil
1 kg (2 lb 4 oz) leg of lamb, cut into bite-sized pieces
1 teaspoon ground ginger
2 onions, each cut into 8 wedges
2 large garlic cloves, crushed
1 cinnamon stick
110 g (3¾ oz/⅔ cup) blanched almonds
1 tablespoon honey
coriander (cilantro) leaves, to garnish

Soak the prunes in 375 ml (13 fl oz/1½ cups) water. Heat half the olive oil in a tagine over medium–high heat. Add the lamb and ginger and cook for 3–4 minutes, turning to brown the lamb on all sides. Remove the lamb to a plate, add the remaining oil to the tagine over medium–low heat, then add the onion and garlic and cook for 5 minutes, or until the onion softens.

Return the lamb to the tagine with the cinnamon stick and the soaking liquid from the prunes. Cover and cook over low heat for 1 hour. Add the prunes and almonds and cook for a further 30 minutes, or until the lamb is very tender. Add the honey and cook for a further 2 minutes, then serve straight from the tagine, sprinkled with coriander.

Artwork by
Benjamin Clarke
mixed media

Chicken, olive and preserved lemon tagine

4 onions, chopped
3 garlic cloves, roughly chopped
1 tablespoon sweet paprika
1 tablespoon ground cumin
2 teaspoons finely grated ginger
1 teaspoon ground turmeric
50 g (1¾ oz/1 cup) chopped fresh coriander (cilantro) leaves and stems,
    plus extra 25 g (1 oz/½ cup) chopped leaves
30 g (1 oz/1 cup) chopped flat-leaf (Italian) parsley
½ teaspoon saffron threads soaked in 1 tablespoon water
60 ml (2 fl oz/¼ cup) olive oil
1 whole chicken, jointed (or use legs and thighs of equal weight)
175 g (6 oz/1 cup) green olives
1 preserved lemon, flesh removed, rind cut into thin segments

Put half the onion in a food processor with the garlic, paprika, cumin, ginger, turmeric, coriander, half the parsley, the saffron mixture and the olive oil and process to make a paste. Rub the paste over the chicken to coat, reserving 2 tablespoons, and refrigerate for at least 30 minutes or overnight.

Spread the reserved paste and remaining onion into the base of a tagine and arrange the chicken over the top, flesh side down. Add the olives and preserved lemon, then pour in 125 ml (4 fl oz/½ cup) water, cover and place over medium heat. Bring to a simmer, but do not boil, then reduce the heat to low and cook for 30 minutes. Turn the chicken over, re-cover and cook for 15–20 minutes, or until the chicken is tender. Serve straight from the tagine, sprinkled with the extra coriander and the remaining parsley.

Pumpkin, eggplant and fennel tagine

80 ml (2½ fl oz/⅓ cup) olive oil
6 small red onions, quartered
2 fennel bulbs, cut in half, core removed and cut into 2 cm (¾ inch) wedges
6 garlic cloves, finely chopped
1 tablespoon ground cumin
1 tablespoon sweet paprika
1 cinnamon stick
600 g (1 lb 5 oz) pumpkin (winter squash), skin left on, seeds removed and
    cut into 1 cm (½ inch) wedges
3 Japanese eggplants (aubergines), cut in half and quartered lengthways
1 litre (35 fl oz/4 cups) vegetable stock
2 bay leaves
150 g (5½ oz/1 cup) pitted kalamata olives
2 tablespoons honey
15 g (½ oz/½ cup) chopped flat-leaf (Italian) parsley
20 g (1 oz/½ cup) chopped coriander (cilantro) leaves

Heat the olive oil in a tagine over medium heat. Add the onion and fennel and cook for about 10 minutes, then add the garlic, cumin, paprika and cinnamon stick and cook for 1–2 minutes — add a little water if you find the mixture is sticking to the tagine. Add the pumpkin, eggplant, vegetable stock and bay leaves, stir well, then cover, reduce the heat to low and cook for about 20 minutes.

Add the olives and honey to the tagine and stir to combine. Cook for a further 10 minutes, or until the vegetables are tender but firm. Season with sea salt and freshly ground black pepper, to taste, and sprinkle over the parsley and coriander to serve.

Carrot and radish salad

3 carrots, sliced into very thin rounds
10 radishes, sliced into very thin rounds
1 tablespoon red wine vinegar
2 tablespoons olive oil
¼ teaspoon ground cinnamon
15 g (½ oz/¼ cup) finely chopped coriander (cilantro) leaves

In a large bowl, mix together the carrot and radish. In a separate bowl, whisk together the red wine vinegar and olive oil and season with cinnamon, sea salt and freshly ground black pepper. Pour the dressing over the carrot and radish mixture and toss through the coriander.

Beetroot and walnut salad

250 g (9 oz) small beetroot (beets)
80 ml (2½ fl oz/⅓ cup) olive oil
60 g (2¼ oz/½ cup) walnuts, toasted and roughly chopped
2 tablespoons finely chopped mint
1½ tablespoons red wine vinegar
½ teaspoon ground cumin
½ teaspoon caster (superfine) sugar

Preheat the oven to 200°C (400°F/Gas 6). Wrap the beetroot in a foil parcel with 2 tablespoons of the olive oil and season with sea salt and freshly ground black pepper. Roast in the oven for 30–40 minutes, or until the beetroot can be pierced easily with a sharp knife but is still firm. Peel off the skins, cut the flesh into small cubes and allow to cool.

Place the beetroot, walnuts and mint in a large bowl and toss to combine.

In a separate bowl, whisk together the remaining olive oil, the vinegar, cumin and sugar. Pour the dressing over the beetroot mixture and toss to coat.

Picnic banquet

The ritual of picnicking is a pastime enjoyed by all — the gathering of people on a grassy knoll, the hunt for the perfect spot to lay the blanket, languid afternoons spent grazing over scattered mixed plates. The following picnic dishes are made up of nibbly little bits, which can be mixed and matched depending on the size of your picnic party, can be transported easily and are perfect to serve at room temperature.

PREPARATION TIME: 1 HOUR 10 MINUTES
  + 1 HOUR 30 MINUTES RISING FOR FOCACCIA DOUGH
  + 1 HOUR REFRIGERATION FOR FRITTER BATTER
COOKING TIME: 30 MINUTES
SERVES: 8

Bocconcini tomato basil sticks

    15 small bocconcini (fresh baby mozzarella cheese) balls
    200 g (7 oz) cherry tomatoes, halved
    15 g (½ oz/½ cup) fresh basil leaves
    1 tablespoon olive oil

Combine the bocconcini with the tomatoes, basil and olive oil in a bowl and season with sea salt and freshly ground black pepper. Set aside to let the flavours infuse for 10 minutes. Thread the bocconcini balls, tomato and basil alternately onto toothpicks. Repeat until all the ingredients are used.

Cucumber and cheese sandwich cut-outs

    butter, for spreading
    10 slices white bread
    cheddar cheese, thinly sliced
    1 Lebanese (short) cucumber, thinly sliced

Lightly butter the bread and assemble the cheese and cucumber over half of the slices. Place the other slices on top to make a sandwich. Using a pastry cutter of your preferred shape, press down firmly on the sandwich to make the shape. Gently remove the cutter and arrange the cut-out shape on a plate or platter.

Artwork by
Felicity Harrold
pencil on paper

Caramelised onion focaccia

5 g (⅛ oz/1½ teaspoons) active dried yeast
1 tablespoon sugar
300 g (10½ oz/2 cups) bread flour, plus extra for kneading
2 tablespoons olive oil, plus extra to oil the bowl
1 teaspoon salt
onion jam (pages 49–50)

Put the yeast, sugar and 185 ml (6 fl oz/¾ cup) warm water in a large bowl and allow to stand for 5 minutes to dissolve the yeast and sugar.

In a large bowl, combine the flour, olive oil and salt. Add the yeast mixture and stir until a soft dough forms. Turn out onto a lightly floured work surface and knead for 8 minutes, or until smooth and elastic — have a little extra flour on the side to use to prevent the dough from sticking to your hands. Place into a large bowl coated lightly with oil, cover and set aside in a warm place for 1 hour, or until the dough has doubled in size.

Punch down the dough, cover and allow to rest for 5 minutes. Gently press the dough into a lightly oiled 20 x 30 cm (8 x 12 inch) baking tin, cover and set aside to rise for 25 minutes, or until almost doubled in size.

Preheat the oven to 180°C (350°F/Gas 4). Spread the onion jam over the dough and bake for 20–25 minutes, or until brown. Cool in the tin for 10 minutes, then remove from the tin and allow to cool completely before serving.

Fig and prosciutto salad

4 cups baby salad greens, washed
½ red onion, thinly sliced
8 figs, sliced into quarters
30 g (1 oz/¼ cup) walnuts, lightly toasted
100 g (3½ oz) prosciutto, torn into strips
200 g (7 oz) goat's cheese
2 tablespoons white balsamic vinegar
60 ml (2 fl oz/¼ cup) olive oil

In a bowl, combine the salad greens, onion, figs, walnuts and prosciutto. Crumble the goat's cheese over the top and toss to combine.

In a small bowl, whisk together the vinegar and olive oil and season with sea salt and freshly ground black pepper, to taste. Pour the dressing over the salad and toss to coat.

Leek and gruyère frittata

3 leeks
2 tablespoons olive oil
20 g (¾ oz) butter
1 garlic clove, finely chopped
8 eggs
60 g (2¼ oz/¾ cup) finely grated gruyère cheese
115 g (4 oz/½ cup) ricotta cheese

Preheat the oven to 180°C (350°F/Gas 4) and grease and line a 23 cm (9 inch) round flan (tart) dish.

Remove and discard the outside skins and the dark green tops of the leeks. Cut the leeks in half lengthways and rinse well under running water to remove all the dirt, then thinly slice crossways.

Heat the olive oil and butter in a large heavy-based frying pan over medium–low heat. Add the leek and garlic and cook for about 8 minutes, or until the leek has softened. Remove from the heat and allow to cool slightly.

In a mixing bowl, whisk together the eggs and gruyère cheese. Add the ricotta and stir gently, leaving the mixture a bit chunky. Add the leek mixture and stir gently until combined. Season with sea salt and freshly ground black pepper, then pour into the prepared dish and cook in the oven for 20 minutes. Place under a preheated grill (broiler) for 3–5 minutes, or until the top is golden. Serve hot, warm or cold.

Sesame seed and parmesan biscuits

225 g (8 oz/1½ cups) plain (all-purpose) flour
200 g (7 oz) butter, chilled and cut into cubes
200 g (7 oz/2 cups) grated parmesan cheese
40 g (1½ oz/¼ cup) sesame seeds

Put the flour and butter into a food processor and process until the mixture resembles breadcrumbs. Transfer to a mixing bowl and add the parmesan and sesame seeds. Use your hands to knead to a smooth dough.

Divide the dough into two evenly-sized portions. Place each portion between two sheets of baking paper and roll out to make rectangles, about 5 mm (¼ inch) thick. Refrigerate for 1 hour.

Preheat the oven to 180°C (350°F/Gas 4). Line a baking tray with baking paper. Cut out circles using a 5 cm (2 inch) pastry cutter. Place the biscuits on the tray and bake for 10–12 minutes, or until golden. Remove from the oven and allow to cool for 5 minutes, before transferring to a wire rack to cool completely.

Sweets and treats

This chapter includes a range of cakes, tarts, puddings and other sweets to team with a cup of tea or coffee, finish off a meal or treat someone on a special occasion. They draw on a range of ingredients, including nuts, chocolate, fresh fruits, such as figs, berries and pears, and a strong presence of citrus flavours. We have a family mantra of 'tastes best with zest'!

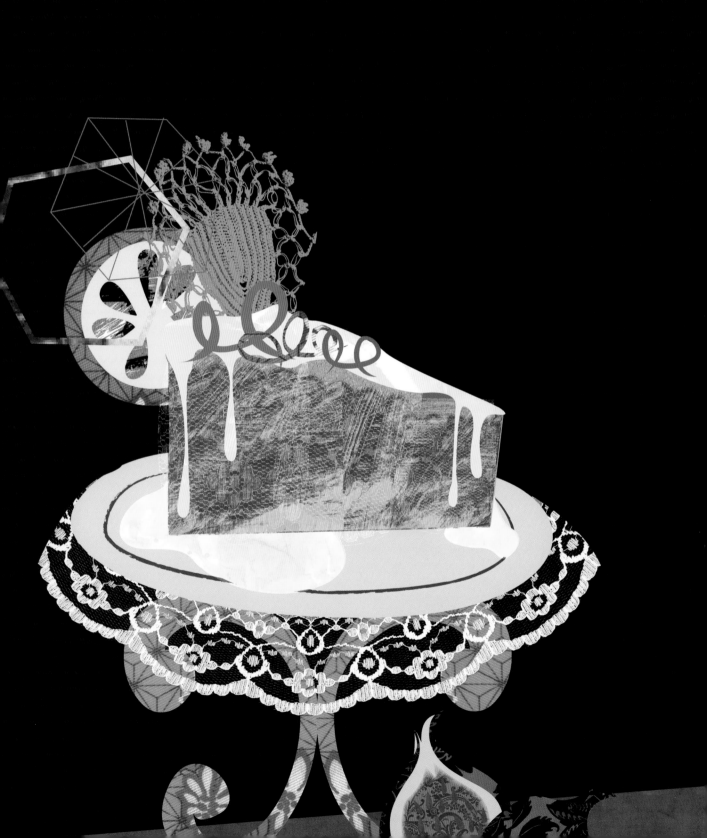

Fig and orange pudding

This is a very earthy, textural dessert with all the telltale signs of a traditional pudding — moist, syrupy and has you sighing after every mouthful! Serve it with some fresh cream or vanilla ice cream, a fireplace and a cup of tea or even a nip of whisky.

PREPARATION TIME: 30 MINUTES + COOLING FIGS
COOKING TIME: 55 MINUTES
SERVES: 4–6

225 g (8 oz) dried figs, finely chopped
125 ml (4 fl oz/½ cup) fresh orange juice
125 g (4½ oz) butter, at room temperature
110 g (3¾ oz/½ cup) caster (superfine) sugar
2 eggs
1 teaspoon finely grated orange zest
110 g (3¾ oz/¾ cup) plain (all-purpose) flour
1½ teaspoons baking powder
55 g (2 oz/½ cup) ground hazelnuts
1 tablespoon Cointreau
115 g (4 oz/⅓ cup) golden syrup (light treacle)

Preheat the oven to 180°C (350°F/Gas 4) and lightly grease a round 18 cm (7 inch) cake tin.

In a small saucepan, combine the figs and orange juice and bring to the boil. Remove from the heat and set aside to cool.

Cream the butter and sugar in a bowl using electric beaters until light and fluffy. Add the eggs, one at a time, beating well after each addition. Add the orange zest and the cooled fig mixture and gently stir to combine. Add the sifted flour and baking powder, ground hazelnuts and Cointreau and mix gently until combined.

Pour the golden syrup evenly into the base of the prepared tin, then pour the pudding mixture over the golden syrup. Place the tin in a deep baking dish and pour enough water into the dish to come halfway up the sides of the tin. Bake in the oven for 30–40 minutes, or until cooked through. Allow the pudding to cool in the tin for 5 minutes, then invert onto a serving plate, cut into wedges and serve warm.

Artwork by
Victoria Topping
digital collage

Pink grapefruit delicious

These individual desserts have all the tangy, juicy sweetness of a pink grapefruit contained in a soft spongy pudding.

PREPARATION TIME: 30 MINUTES + 4–6 HOURS DRYING PEEL
COOKING TIME: 1 HOUR 50 MINUTES
SERVES: 6

CANDIED PEEL
1 pink grapefruit, peeled
220 g (7¾ oz/1 cup) caster (superfine) sugar, plus extra to coat

PUDDINGS
90 g (3¼ oz) butter, at room temperature
150 g (5½ oz/⅔ cup) caster (superfine) sugar
3 teaspoons finely grated pink grapefruit zest
3 eggs, separated
100 g (3½ oz/⅔ cup) plain (all-purpose) flour
1½ teaspoons baking powder
420 ml (14½ fl oz/1⅔ cups) milk
125 ml (4 fl oz/½ cup) grapefruit juice
icing (confectioners') sugar, to dust
cream or ice cream, to serve

To make the candied peel, top and tail the grapefruit. Score the skin in quarters, cutting only through the peel and pith, not into the fruit. Peel off the rind, removing any white pith, and cut into 5 mm (¼ inch) wide strips. Place the peel in a saucepan of cold water, bring to the boil, then drain and rinse the peel. Repeat another two or three times — the more you do it, the less tart it will be.

Put the sugar and 250 ml (9 fl oz/1 cup) water in a saucepan over medium–high heat, stirring until the sugar has dissolved. Bring to the boil, then reduce the heat to low. Add the peel and simmer for 1 hour, or until the peel is shiny and translucent. Remove with a slotted spoon and place on a wire rack to dry, about 4–6 hours. Dust liberally with caster sugar and store in an airtight container until ready to serve.

To make the puddings, preheat the oven to 180°C (350°F/Gas 4) and lightly grease six 250 ml (9 fl oz/1 cup) capacity ramekins. Put the butter, sugar and grapefruit zest in a bowl and use electric beaters to cream them together until light and fluffy. Add the egg yolks, one at a time, beating well after each addition. Fold in the sifted flour and baking powder alternately with the milk to make a smooth batter.

Using electric beaters, whisk the egg whites in a clean bowl until stiff peaks form. Gently fold the egg whites into the batter with the grapefruit juice until just combined. Pour the mixture into the prepared ramekins and place the ramekins in a deep baking dish. Pour enough water into the dish to come halfway up the sides of the ramekins and cook in the oven for about 40 minutes, varying the cooking time in accordance with how runny you like your puddings. Remove from the oven, dust the tops lightly with icing sugar and top with some candied grapefruit peel. Serve with cream or ice cream, if desired.

Artwork by
Mark Lazenby
digital illustration

Chocolate mousse

A staple in any 1980s cookbook next to dishes such as lobster thermidore and frozen daiquiris, chocolate mousse is known for its somewhat sensual, kitsch demeanour. Whip it good.

PREPARATION TIME: 20 MINUTES + 3 HOURS REFRIGERATION
COOKING TIME: 5 MINUTES
SERVES: 6

> 200 g (7 oz) dark chocolate, chopped
> 3 eggs, separated
> 300 ml (10½ fl oz) thickened (whipping)
>   cream, lightly whipped
> 1 tablespoon brandy or Grand Marnier

Put the chocolate in a heatproof bowl. Set the bowl over a saucepan of just simmering water, making sure the base of the bowl doesn't touch the water. Stir until the chocolate has melted, then remove from the heat. Rapidly stir in the egg yolks to avoid them from setting, then stir in the cream and brandy.

In a large clean dry bowl, whisk the egg whites using electric beaters until soft peaks form. Gently fold the chocolate mixture into the egg whites, using a large metal spoon.

Divide the mousse among serving glasses and refrigerate for at least 3 hours or overnight to allow them to set before serving.

Artwork by
Beastman
digital illustration

Lemon polenta cake

This is a simple, dreamy cake — buttery and grainy with a citrus tang. Given the grain and nut content, you could even get away with having a slice for breakfast.

PREPARATION TIME: 30 MINUTES
COOKING TIME: 40 MINUTES
SERVES: 10

300 g (10½ oz) butter, softened
300 g (10½ oz/1⅓ cups) caster (superfine) sugar
4 eggs
300 g (10½ oz/3 cups) almond meal
190 g (6¾ oz/1 cup) polenta
1 teaspoon baking powder
300 ml (10½ fl oz) lemon juice (from about 5 large lemons)
1 tablespoon finely grated lemon zest
icing (confectioners') sugar, for dusting

Preheat the oven to 160°C (315°F/Gas 2–3). Lightly grease a round 20 cm (8 inch) cake tin and line the base and side with baking paper.

Cream the butter and sugar in a large bowl using electric beaters until light and fluffy. Add the eggs, one at a time, beating well after each addition.

In a separate bowl, mix together the almond meal, polenta and baking powder. Fold through the egg mixture and mix until well combined. Add the lemon juice and zest and stir well, then pour into the prepared tin.

Bake the cake in the oven for 40 minutes, or until a skewer inserted into the centre of the cake comes out clean. Remove from the oven and allow to cool in the tin for at least 10 minutes, before inverting carefully onto a plate. Dust with the icing sugar, cut into slices and serve.

Artwork by
Joe Baker
digital illustration

Courgette cake

This cake was first introduced to us by our friend, Daisy, in the UK. It has since been a feature at many picnics, birthdays and tea parties. Like its cousin the carrot cake, the courgette helps to make the cake moist and sweet.

PREPARATION TIME: 30 MINUTES + 10 MINUTES DRAINING
COOKING TIME: 30 MINUTES
SERVES: 8

250 g (9 oz) zucchini (courgettes), grated
125 ml (4 fl oz/½ cup) sunflower oil
2 eggs
150 g (5½ oz/⅔ cup) caster (superfine) sugar
225 g (8 oz/1½ cups) self-raising flour
½ teaspoon bicarbonate of soda (baking soda)
½ teaspoon baking powder
finely grated zest of 1 lime
juice of 1 lime

FILLING
200 g (7 oz) cream cheese, at room temperature
90 g (3¼ oz/¾ cup) icing (confectioners') sugar,
    sifted, plus extra for dusting
finely grated zest of 1 lime
juice of 1 lime
200 g (7 oz/1⅓ cups) pistachios, roughly chopped

Preheat the oven to 180°C (350°F/Gas 4). Lightly grease two round 20 cm (8 inch) cake tins and line the bases with baking paper. Coarsely grate the zucchini, place in a colander and sprinkle with salt. Allow to sit for 10 minutes, then squeeze out the excess moisture.

Put the sunflower oil, eggs and sugar into a large bowl and whisk until creamy. Sift in the flour, bicarbonate of soda and baking powder and stir until well combined. Stir in the grated zucchini, lime zest and lime juice and mix until just combined.

Divide the mixture evenly between the prepared tins and bake in the oven for 30 minutes, or until firm to the touch and golden. Leave to cool for 10 minutes, then remove the cakes from their tins and transfer to a wire rack to cool completely.

To make the filling, combine the cream cheese, icing sugar, lime zest and lime juice and mix until smooth and well combined. Stir in the pistachios, cover, and set aside at room temperature until ready to use.

Spread the cream cheese filling thickly over the top of one of the cakes. Top with the second cake and dust with icing sugar. Cut into generous slices to serve.

Artwork by
Inés Iglesias
watercolour on paper

Earl Grey teacake

Earl Grey teacake literally uses a good old cup of Earl Grey tea for the liquid component, infusing the sponge with the exotic flavour of bergamot. Crispy and buttery on the outside, moist and fluffy on the inside, this cake is great served hot, warm or cold, with or without butter.

PREPARATION TIME: 30 MINUTES
COOKING TIME: 1 HOUR
SERVES: 10

150 g (5½ oz) butter, at room temperature
225 g (8 oz/1¼ cups) soft brown sugar
3 eggs
225 g (8 oz/1½ cups) plain (all-purpose) flour, sifted
2 teaspoons baking powder
50 g (1¾ oz/½ cup) almond meal
2 tablespoons Earl Grey tea leaves
170 ml (5½ fl oz/⅔ cup) strong Earl Grey tea, brewed
    fresh from leaves and cooled

Preheat the oven to 180°C (350°F/Gas 4). Lightly grease a deep 9 x 22 cm (3½ x 8½ inch) loaf (bar) tin and line the base with baking paper.

Cream the butter and sugar in a bowl using electric beaters until light and fluffy. Add the eggs one at a time, beating well after each addition. Combine the sifted flour, baking powder, almond meal and tea leaves and add to the butter mixture, alternately with the brewed tea, making sure you mix thoroughly after each addition to make a smooth batter.

Pour the batter into the prepared tin and bake in the oven for 1 hour, or until a skewer inserted into the centre of the cake comes out clean. Leave in the tin to cool for 5 minutes before turning out onto a wire rack to cool completely.

Serve the teacake with a big pot of freshly brewed tea.

Artwork by
Mump
digital illustration

Flourless chocolate cake

For this cake we recommend buying whole nuts and grinding them yourself, which adds more body and texture. We have used only almonds, as well as different combinations of almonds with hazelnuts, sunflower seeds and pine nuts. You can use just about any nuts and seeds you have on hand, which will give the cake a slightly different flavour each time.

PREPARATION TIME: 30 MINUTES
COOKING TIME: 50 MINUTES
SERVES: 12

150 g (5½ oz) blanched almonds
100 g (3½ oz) raw mixed nuts, such as macadamias,
  hazelnuts, pistachios, pine nuts or even sunflower seeds
200 g (7 oz/1⅓ cups) chopped dark chocolate
200 g (7 oz) butter, cut into cubes
220 g (7¾ oz/1 cup) caster (superfine) sugar
5 eggs, separated
a pinch of salt
finely grated zest of 1 lemon
icing (confectioners') sugar, for dusting

GRAND MARNIER MASCARPONE
250 g (9 oz) mascarpone
1 tablespoon Grand Marnier or soft brown sugar

Preheat the oven to 180°C (350°F/Gas 4). Lightly grease a round 23 cm (9 inch) cake tin and line the base with baking paper. Place all of the nuts and seeds into a food processor and process until fine.

Place the chocolate into a heatproof bowl set over a saucepan of simmering water, making sure the base of the bowl doesn't touch the water. Stir until the chocolate has melted, then add the butter and stir until it has melted. Add the sugar and stir until it has dissolved and the mixture is smooth and glossy. Remove from the heat and cool slightly, then add the egg yolks, beating quickly to prevent them from cooking. Stir in the processed nuts.

Beat the egg whites and salt in a large clean dry bowl using electric beaters until soft peaks form. Add the lemon zest and gently fold in the chocolate mixture, using a large metal spoon, to just combine — avoid overmixing. Pour into the prepared tin and bake in the oven for 35–45 minutes, or until a skewer inserted into the centre of the cake comes out clean. Remove from the oven and allow to cool in the tin for 10 minutes before turning out onto a wire rack to cool completely.

To make the Grand Marnier mascarpone, whisk together the mascarpone and Grand Marnier until well combined.

Dust the cooled cake with icing sugar, cut into wedges and serve with a dollop of the Grand Marnier mascarpone on the side.

Artwork by
Teebs
mixed media on canvas

Yes

spork   knife

NO

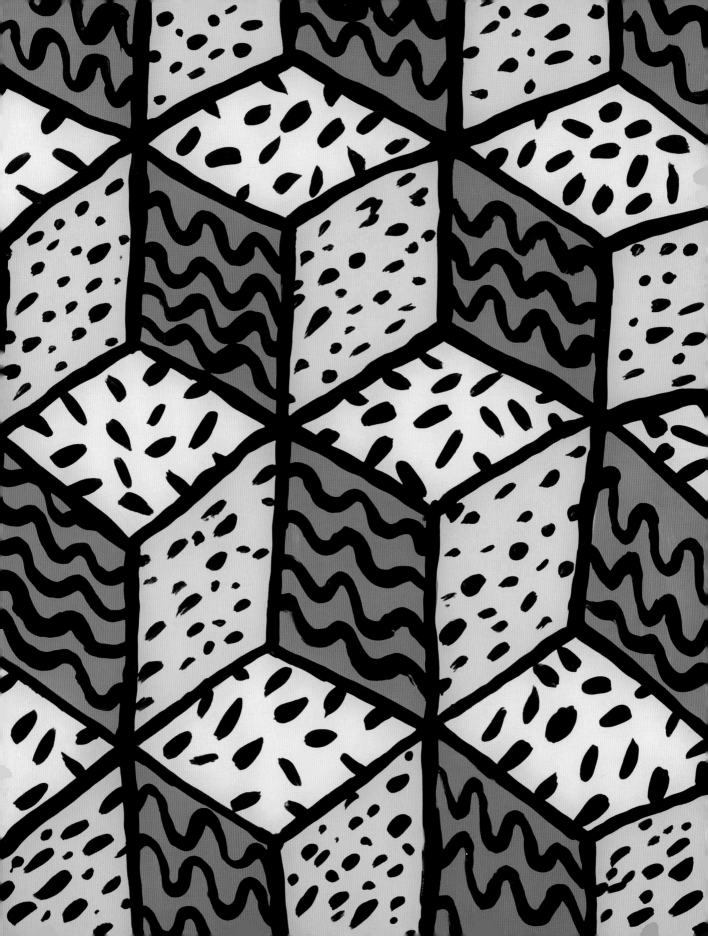

Jam and coconut slice

The simplicity and hardiness of slices make them perfect for bakers of all ages and skill sets. This slice is loved for its chewy coconut topping, sweet jam and buttery, crumbly base. You can use different flavours of jam — strawberry, blackberry and apricot work well too.

PREPARATION TIME: 20 MINUTES
COOKING TIME: 30 MINUTES
MAKES: 20 PIECES

300 g (10½ oz/2 cups) plain (all-purpose) flour
220 g (7¾ oz/1 cup) caster (superfine) sugar
200 g (7 oz) butter, cut into cubes
4 eggs
250 g (9 oz/¾ cup) raspberry jam
200 g (7 oz/3 cups) shredded coconut

Preheat the oven to 180°C (350°F/Gas 4). Lightly grease an 18 x 28 cm (7 x 11¼ inch) baking tin and line with baking paper.

Combine the sifted flour and 110 g (3¾ oz/½ cup) of the sugar in a mixing bowl. Use your fingertips to rub in the butter until well combined. Alternatively, use a food processor to combine the ingredients. Add one lightly beaten egg and mix to form a soft dough. Press the mixture into the prepared tin.

Spread the jam evenly over the base — if the jam you are using has a thick consistency, it can be warmed in a saucepan or in a microwave to make it easier to spread.

Using a fork or whisk, beat the remaining sugar and eggs together in a small bowl until the mixture is pale. Stir in the coconut to combine, then spread over the jam.

Bake the slice in the oven for 25–30 minutes, or until the coconut topping is golden brown. Remove from the oven and leave the slice to cool in the tin. Cut into pieces and serve.

Artwork by
Billie Justice Thomson
acrylic on perspex

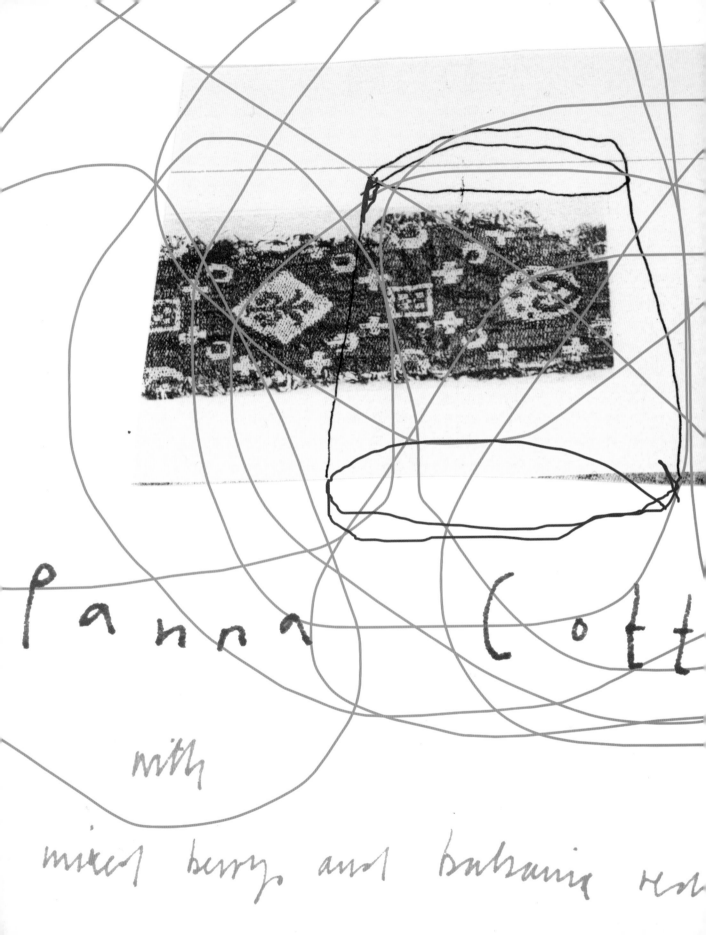

panna Cott

with

mixed berry and balsamic red

Panna cotta with berry balsamic reduction

Delicate and refined, panna cotta may seem daunting to make. Once you master the gelatine component of this dessert, you can constantly reinvent the flavour by adding different ingredients, such as green tea powder, chocolate, coffee, blood orange or coconut.

PREPARATION TIME: 30 MINUTES + 2 HOURS REFRIGERATION
COOKING TIME: 25 MINUTES
SERVES: 6

3 teaspoons powdered gelatine
500 ml (17 fl oz/2 cups) pouring (whipping) cream
55 g (2 oz/¼ cup) caster (superfine) sugar
1 vanilla bean, split lengthways and seeds scraped, or
   1 teaspoon natural vanilla extract

BERRY BALSAMIC REDUCTION
125 g (4½ oz/1 cup) mixed fresh or frozen berries
125 ml (4 fl oz/½ cup) balsamic vinegar
55 g (2 oz/¼ cup) caster (superfine) sugar

Lightly oil six 125 ml (4 fl oz/½ cup) capacity ramekins. Put 2 tablespoons of hot water in a large bowl and sprinkle over the gelatine. Whisk to dissolve the gelatine and allow to sit for 5 minutes.

Heat the cream and sugar in a saucepan over medium heat until just below boiling point. Once the sugar has dissolved, remove from the heat and stir in the vanilla seeds or extract. Set aside.

Pour the warm panna cotta mixture over the gelatine and whisk until the gelatine has completely dissolved. Divide the mixture into the ramekins, then refrigerate until firm, at least 2 hours or preferably overnight.

To make the berry balsamic reduction, put all of the ingredients into a small saucepan over medium–low heat and cook for 15–20 minutes, stirring occasionally to ensure the berries do not burn — the mixture is ready when the sugar has completely dissolved and the sauce begins to thicken slightly.

Turn the panna cotta onto serving plates and drizzle generously with the berry balsamic reduction. Serve immediately.

Artwork by
Gabrielle Herzog
mixed media

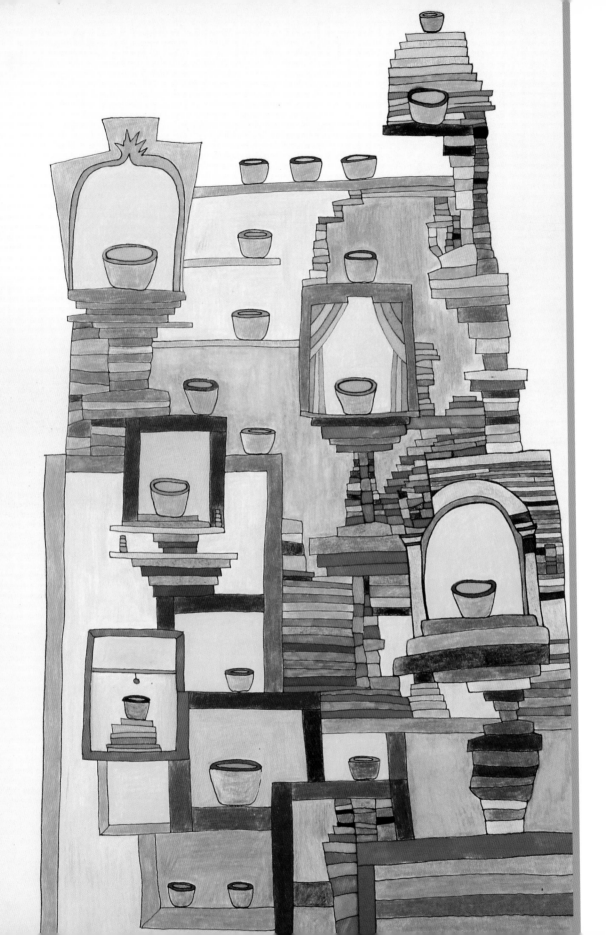

Portuguese custard tarts

The enticing smell of baking custard and warm pastry makes it hard to resist these tarts fresh out of the oven, but try and limit yourself, as they are best enjoyed cold and wrinkly!

PREPARATION TIME: 30 MINUTES + COOLING
COOKING TIME: 40 MINUTES
MAKES: 8

3 egg yolks
125 g (4½ oz) caster (superfine) sugar
2 tablespoons cornflour (cornstarch)
375 ml (13 fl oz/1½ cups) milk
2 cm (¾ inch) strip lemon rind, white pith removed
1 cinnamon stick
170 g (6 oz/1 sheet) frozen puff pastry, defrosted

Put the egg yolks, sugar and cornflour in a saucepan and whisk until well combined. Add the milk, whisking to combine, then add the lemon rind and cinnamon stick and place over medium–low heat. Continuously whisk the mixture as it heats, making sure to get into all the edges of the pan to ensure a smooth custard. Continue whisking for 5–7 minutes, or until the custard thickens enough to coat the back of a wooden spoon — it will thicken suddenly, so watch it carefully and whisk constantly. Remove the pan from the heat, strain into a bowl, discarding the lemon rind and cinnamon stick. Cover with plastic wrap to prevent a skin forming, and set aside to cool.

Preheat the oven to 220°C (425°F/Gas 7). Grease an eight-hole 125 ml (4 fl oz/ ½ cup) capacity muffin tin. While the custard is cooling, make the tart shells. Cut the pastry sheet in half, lay one piece on top of the other and let sit for a few minutes to fuse. Roll the pastry tightly into a cylinder from the short end to make a 12 cm (4½ inch) cylinder. Cut the cylinder into eight rounds. Using a rolling pin, flatten each round into a 9 cm (3½ inch) circle.

Push each pastry circle into a muffin hole. Divide the custard evenly between the pastry shells. Bake in the oven for 20–25 minutes, or until golden brown. If the tarts don't brown you can place them for a brief moment under a preheated griller (broiler), but be careful not to burn the pastry. Cool in the tin for about 5 minutes, then remove to a wire rack to cool.

Artwork by
Erin Lightfoot
pencil on paper

Sticky date and ginger pudding with butterscotch sauce

An eternal favourite, this pudding has been winning hearts for generations. This version is spiced up with some fresh ginger.

PREPARATION TIME: 30 MINUTES + 15 MINUTES SOAKING
COOKING TIME: 35 MINUTES
SERVES: 6–8

250 g (9 oz) pitted dates, roughly chopped
1 teaspoon bicarbonate of soda (baking soda)
375 ml (13 fl oz/1½ cups) boiling water
90 g (3¼ oz) butter, at room temperature
165 g (5¾ oz/¾ cup) caster (superfine) sugar
2 eggs
1 teaspoon finely grated ginger
250 g (9 oz/1⅔ cups) self-raising flour
1 tablespoon ground ginger
ice cream, to serve

BUTTERSCOTCH SAUCE
250 ml (9 fl oz/1 cup) pouring (whipping) cream
100 g (3½ oz) butter, chopped
185 g (6½ oz/1 cup) soft brown sugar

Heat the oven to 180°C (350°F/Gas 4). Lightly grease a square or round 20 cm (8 inch) baking dish. Combine the dates and bicarbonate of soda in a bowl. Pour over the boiling water, stir well, and set aside for 15 minutes for the dates to soften and the mixture to cool.

In a separate bowl, cream the butter and sugar using electric beaters until light and fluffy. Add the eggs one at a time, beating well after each addition, then stir in the grated ginger. Fold in the combined sifted flour and ground ginger, then gently stir in the cooled date mixture. Pour into the prepared dish and cook in the oven for about 30 minutes, or until firm to the touch.

Meanwhile, make the butterscotch sauce. Combine the cream, butter and sugar in a small saucepan over medium heat. Stir until the butter has melted and the sugar has dissolved, then reduce the heat to low and simmer for a further 3–4 minutes, or until the sauce has thickened slightly.

Remove the pudding from the oven, make incisions in the top with a point of a knife and slowly pour over some of the sauce, reserving half to serve. Return the pudding to the oven for 2 minutes to allow the sauce to soak in, then cut into wedges and serve hot with ice cream or yoghurt and the reserved warm butterscotch sauce.

Artwork by
Rhiannon McLay
watercolour on paper

Very gingery gingernuts

These spicy little numbers are perfect for tea-dunking.

PREPARATION TIME: 30 MINUTES
COOKING TIME: 30 MINUTES
MAKES: 40 BISCUITS

250 g (9 oz) butter, chopped
185 g (6½ oz/1 cup) soft brown sugar
175 g (6 oz/½ cup) golden syrup (light treacle)
3 tablespoons ground ginger
1 teaspoon ground cinnamon
1 teaspoon bicarbonate of soda (baking soda)
1 tablespoon boiling water
450 g (1 lb/3 cups) plain (all-purpose) flour, sifted

Preheat the oven to 180°C (350°F/Gas 4). Line two baking trays with baking paper.

Combine the butter, sugar, golden syrup, ginger and cinnamon in a saucepan over medium heat, stirring frequently until the butter has melted. Remove from the heat.

Put the bicarbonate of soda in a bowl with the boiling water and stir to dissolve. Add to the butter mixture and stir well. Add the flour and use a flat-bladed knife to mix and form a soft dough.

Roll the mixture into walnut-sized balls and arrange on the prepared trays. Flatten slightly into discs, making sure there are a few centimetres between each biscuit. Bake the gingernuts in the oven for 15–20 minutes, or until the biscuits are deep golden brown. Remove from the oven and transfer to a wire rack to cool.

Artwork by
James Kape
digital collage

Apple and rhubarb crostata

This country-style crostata features sweet and tangy rhubarb encased in buttery crumbly pastry. Use the pastry from the seasonal fruit tart recipe and add a little lemon zest for an extra citrus twist.

PREPARATION TIME: 45 MINUTES
+ 2 HOURS REFRIGERATION FOR PASTRY + COOLING FOR FRUIT
COOKING TIME: 1 HOUR 20 MINUTES
SERVES: 10-12

1 quantity sweet shortcrust pastry (pages 203–204)

FILLING
500 g (1 lb 2 oz) rhubarb, trimmed and cut into 2 cm (¾ inch) pieces
300 g (10½ oz/about 3) apples, peeled, cored and cut into chunks
150 g (5½ oz/⅔ cup) caster (superfine) sugar, plus extra for dusting
1 vanilla bean, split lengthways and seeds scraped
pouring (whipping) cream or ice cream, to serve

To make the filling, combine the rhubarb, apple, sugar and vanilla seeds in a large saucepan over medium heat. Cook for 20 minutes, or until the fruit starts to break down, stirring frequently to prevent it sticking and burning. Remove from the heat and set aside to cool.

Preheat the oven to 200°C (400°F/Gas 6) and lightly grease a round 25 cm (10 inch) pie dish, about 3 cm (1¼ inches) deep. Remove the pastry from the refrigerator and leave for about 20 minutes to soften, then divide into one-quarter and three-quarter portions. Place the larger portion of pastry on a lightly floured work surface or between two sheets of baking paper. Using a rolling pin, roll the pastry into a circle large enough to fit the pie dish, then transfer the pastry to the dish. Line the pastry shell with baking paper and pastry weights (you can also use uncooked rice, lentils or beans) and cook in the oven for about 15 minutes, or until just golden. Remove from the oven, remove the paper and pastry weights and set aside to cool.

Reduce the oven temperature to 180°C (350°F/Gas 4). Roll out the remaining dough between two sheets of baking paper into a circle with a 29 cm (11½ inch) diameter. Cut the circle into strips about 1 cm (½ inch) wide. Transfer the strips on the baking paper to a plate and refrigerate until ready to use.

Fill the pastry shell with the cooled rhubarb mixture and top with the pastry strips to make a lattice pattern. Brush the pastry with a little milk and sprinkle with a little extra sugar. Bake in the oven for 35–40 minutes, or until the pastry is golden brown and the fruit juices are bubbling. Serve hot or warm with cream or ice cream.

artwork by
Funny Banana
embroidery

THEOBROMA CACAO - *COCOA BEAN*

Chocolate truffle assortment

These decadent balls hit the spot for even the most dedicated chocolate fiend. In addition to a more traditional truffle version, we've provided Mexican and Japanese versions. Matcha powder is a green tea powder and is available at most Asian grocery stores. This assortment can be served together or individually, depending on the occasion. You can also experiment with other spices, nuts and liqueurs.

PREPARATION TIME: 20 MINUTES + 2 HOURS REFRIGERATION
COOKING TIME: 5 MINUTES
MAKES: 30 SMALL TRUFFLES

400 g (14 oz) dark chocolate (70% cocoa solids)
125 ml (4 fl oz/½ cup) pouring (whipping) cream
unsweetened cocoa powder, for dusting

LIQUEUR
1 tablespoon brandy

MEXICAN
1 tablespoon instant coffee powder
1 teaspoon natural vanilla extract
1 teaspoon ground cinnamon
1 teaspoon cayenne pepper

JAPANESE
1 teaspoon matcha powder, plus extra for dusting

Break the chocolate into small pieces in a large bowl. Add the cream to a small saucepan and bring almost to the boil. Pour the hot cream over the chocolate and add your preferred flavourings — liqueur, Mexican spices or matcha powder. Stir until the ingredients are well combined and the mixture is smooth. Cover and refrigerate for 1–1½ hours to set.

Using a teaspoon, take a bite-sized piece of the chocolate mixture and roll into a small ball. Repeat with the remaining mixture. If you are making the liqueur or Mexican truffles, spread the cocoa on a plate. If you are making Japanese truffles spread the matcha powder on a plate. Roll individual truffles in powder to coat, then transfer to a serving plate and refrigerate until ready to serve.

Artwork by
Kirsten Williamson
pencil on paper

Coconut macaroons

Unlike the impeccable French macaroon, these haphazard haystacks of coconut are deliciously imperfect. They are simple and quick enough to whip up at the last minute when surprise guests drop round, or if you have a 'must-satisfy-now' sweet craving.

PREPARATION TIME: 20 MINUTES
COOKING TIME: 15 MINUTES
MAKES: 30–40 BISCUITS

> 4 egg whites, at room temperature
> ¼ teaspoon salt
> 165 g (5¾ oz/¾ cup) caster (superfine) sugar
> 1 teaspoon natural vanilla extract
> 200 g (7 oz/3 cups) shredded coconut

Preheat the oven to 180°C (350°F/Gas 4). Line two large baking trays with baking paper.

Beat the egg whites and salt in a clean dry bowl using electric beaters until soft peaks form. Add the sugar, a spoonful at a time, beating well after each addition. Mix for a further 2 minutes, or until the mixture is thick and glossy. Add the vanilla extract and whisk to combine, then gently fold in the coconut using a metal spoon.

Spoon tablespoons of the mixture onto the prepared trays, leaving about 2 cm (¾ inch) between each as they will spread when cooked. Bake in the oven for 12–15 minutes, or until light golden and firm. Remove from the oven and allow to cool on the trays for 5 minutes, before transferring to a wire rack to cool completely.

Artwork by
James Dodd
mixed media

Dessert platter

This smorgasbord of decadence takes no prisoners, serving up chocolate, cheese, battered fruit, nuts and candied peel. While you're at it, you may as well top it off with a brandy or cognac tipple.

PREPARATION TIME: 2 HOURS + 4–6 HOURS DRYING PEEL + REFRIGERATION
COOKING TIME: 1 HOUR
SERVES: 10+

Honeyed figs with gorgonzola

10 fresh figs
200 g (7 oz) gorgonzola cheese
115 g (4 oz/⅓ cup) honey, warmed

Preheat the oven to 180°C (350°F/Gas 4) and line a baking tray with baking paper. Using a sharp knife, make a cross-shaped incision in the top of each fig, about 5 mm (¼ inch) deep. Gently pry the edges apart and stuff each fig with about 1 teaspoon of the gorgonzola. Place the figs upright on the tray and bake in the oven until the figs are plump and just soft, about 10 minutes. Drizzle the figs with honey and top with a little freshly ground black pepper.

Dark chocolate orange peel

2 oranges
220 g (7¾ oz/1 cup) caster (superfine) sugar
100 g (3½ oz/⅔ cup) chopped dark chocolate

Top and tail the oranges. Score the skin of each orange in quarters, cutting only through the peel, not into the fruit. Peel off the rind, removing any white pith, and cut into 5 mm (¼ inch) wide strips. Place the peel in a saucepan of cold water, bring to the boil, then drain and rinse the peel. Repeat another two or three times — the more you do it, the less tart the peel will be.

Put the sugar and 250 ml (9 fl oz/1 cup) water in a saucepan over medium–high heat, stirring until the sugar has dissolved. Bring to the boil, then reduce the heat to low, add the peel and simmer for 1 hour, or until the peel is shiny and translucent. Remove with a slotted spoon and place on a wire rack to dry, about 4–6 hours.

Place the chocolate in a heatproof bowl over a saucepan of simmering water, making sure the base of the bowl does not touch the water. Stir until the chocolate melts. Dip the orange peel in the chocolate and then place on a sheet of baking paper to dry completely before serving.

Artwork by
Lucy James
digital collage

Cinnamon nuts

1 egg white
200 g (7 oz/1½ cups) mixed raw nuts
2 tablespoons caster (superfine) sugar
½ teaspoon ground cinnamon
¼ teaspoon salt

Preheat the oven to 100°C (200°F/Gas ½) and lightly grease a baking tray. Lightly beat the egg white in a large clean dry bowl until frothy but not stiff. Add the nuts and stir until well coated.

In a separate large bowl, combine the sugar, cinnamon and salt. Remove the nuts from the egg mixture and place into the sugar mixture, tossing to coat. Spread the nuts in an even layer on the baking tray and bake in the oven for 45 minutes, stirring occasionally, until golden. Allow to cool before serving.

Peach fritters

185 ml (6 fl oz/¾ cup) sweet sparkling wine
2 eggs, separated
110 g (3¾ oz/¾ cup) plain (all-purpose) flour
2 teaspoons caster (superfine) sugar
a pinch of salt
grapeseed oil, for deep-frying
2 peaches, halved, stones removed
    and cut into 1.5 cm (⅝ inch) wedges
lemon wedges, to serve

Combine the wine, egg yolks, flour, sugar and salt in a large bowl and beat well to form a smooth thick batter. Cover with plastic wrap and refrigerate for 1 hour.

Whisk the egg whites and a pinch of salt in a clean dry bowl using electric beaters until stiff peaks form. Fold the whites through the batter mixture.

Fill a large heavy-based saucepan with enough grapeseed oil so that it comes about 4 cm (1½ inches) up the side of the pan and place over medium–high heat — the oil is hot enough when a little batter dropped into the oil bubbles furiously. Dip the peach wedges into the batter to coat and then lower them, in batches, into the hot oil. Deep-fry for 1–2 minutes, or until golden. Remove the fritters and place on a plate lined with paper towel.

Serve the peach fritters immediately with lemon wedges on the side.

Seasonal fruit tart

For this decorative tart you can use almost any seasonal fruit, such as quinces, pears, peaches and apples. If you are making your own pastry it will need to cool in the refrigerator for at least 1 hour, so factor this extra time into your baking schedule. Try to handle the dough as little as possible for best results.

PREPARATION TIME: 1 HOUR
 + 2 HOURS 15 MINUTES RESTING FOR SHORTCRUST PASTRY
COOKING TIME: 1 HOUR 40 MINUTES
SERVES: 12

SWEET SHORTCRUST PASTRY
260 g (9¼ oz/1¾ cups) plain (all-purpose) flour
30 g (1 oz/¼ cup) icing (confectioners') sugar
180 g (6½ oz) chilled butter, chopped
1 egg yolk, lightly whisked

POACHED SEASONAL FRUIT
500 ml (17 fl oz/2 cups) rosé wine
110 g (3¾ oz/½ cup) sugar
1 cinnamon stick
2 star anise
6 whole cloves
6 whole black peppercorns
4–6 pieces fruit, peeled, cored and halved or quartered

FRANGIPANE FILLING
200 g (7 oz) butter, at room temperature
220 g (7¾ oz/1 cup) caster (superfine) sugar
200 g (7 oz/2 cups) almond meal
2 eggs
2 tablespoons plain (all-purpose) flour
2 tablespoons brandy
1 vanilla bean, split lengthways and seeds scraped
vanilla ice cream or thickened cream, to serve

To make the pastry, combine the flour, icing sugar and butter in a food processor and process until the mixture resembles breadcrumbs (you can do this by hand — use your fingers to evenly distribute the butter). Add the egg yolk and enough iced water to just bring the pastry together. Turn out onto a lightly floured work surface and knead lightly until just smooth. Bring into a ball, then flatten into a disc shape, wrap in plastic wrap and refrigerate for at least 2 hours.

CONTINUED ➔➔

To make the poached fruit, combine the wine, sugar, spices and 500 ml (17 fl oz/ 2 cups) water in a saucepan over high heat. Cover and bring to the boil, then reduce the heat and simmer for 10 minutes. Add the fruit pieces, cover and simmer for a further 10–30 minutes, depending on the variety and ripeness of the fruit — the flesh should be tender but still firm when done. Use a slotted spoon to remove the fruit from the pan and set aside to cool. Increase the heat to high and continue to boil the poaching syrup until about 125 ml (4 fl oz/½ cup) remains — the more you reduce it, the richer the syrup becomes.

To make the frangipane filling, beat the butter, sugar and almond meal in a bowl using electric beaters. Add the eggs, one at a time, beating well after each addition. Stir in the flour, brandy and vanilla seeds using a metal spoon until well combined.

Preheat the oven to 200°C (400°F/Gas 6). Lightly grease a loose-based 27 cm (10¾ inch) round fluted flan (tart) tin. Roll out the pastry on a lightly floured work surface to make a circle large enough to line the tin. Lower the pastry into the tin, pressing into the sides and trim any excess. Refrigerate for 15 minutes.

Line the pastry shell with a layer of baking paper and some baking weights (you can also use dry rice, lentils or beans) and blind bake for 15–20 minutes, or until golden. Remove from the oven and allow the pastry to cool slightly.

Reduce the oven temperature to 180°C (350°F/Gas 4). Spread the frangipane filling evenly into the pastry. Dig little 'nests' in the filling and place the cooled poached fruit inside. Bake the tart in the oven for 30–40 minutes, or until golden brown. Remove from the oven and allow to cool in the tin.

Cut into wedges and serve hot or cold with vanilla ice cream or cream and some of the poaching syrup.

artwork by
Jade Borjesson
coloured pencil on paper

Author Biographies

Jessica Thompson

Thankfully, Jess's cooking skills have developed since the time she made Anzac biscuits at age five, and assumed that 3/4 teaspoon of bicarbonate of soda was a misprint for 3/4 cup. At 13 she cooked up her first banquet for family friends – an Indian feast prepared on a one-ring gas camping stove and a convection microwave.

After studying marketing and linguistics, Jess has worked in communications roles for various arts, cultural & travel companies. She collaborates content for The Bookery Cook blog, loves platters, pottering in the garden and lengthy kitchen sessions. New places, food and produce always excite her – whether it's shopping at a local market or a corner store, eating fish and chips or fine dining, getting cooking lessons from Japanese neighbours or learning how to cure pork in New Zealand. 'Shirako sarada' – a Japanese 'salad' of raw fish sperm tubes – has been her most challenging food moment to date.

Georgia Thompson

Georgie has always been passionate about food and the adventures that come with it. Growing up in a tropical hinterland with her sisters, days were spent exploring the surrounding mango, pineapple and avocado farmland. This encouraged a love of travelling and experiencing cultures through food.

Keeping her professional and personal projects as varied as her palate, in addition to The Bookery Cook, Georgie works as a freelance digital designer and busies herself in her spare time with DJing. With a degree in interactive design, she's passionate about design - recognising it as a tool for communication, collaboration and innovation.

A self-confessed 'better eater than cook', you're mostly likely to find her tucking into a big bowl of steamed mussels, collaborating on new projects and dreaming up what her next food-related adventure will be.

Maxine Thompson

Maxie's first venture into a professional kitchen was at the age of eighteen when she was managing and cooking at a beachside café, where her famous muffins (Max's muff) became the hottest menu item in town. Her cooking craze continued globally moving on to work at one of Bristol's finest Mexican Restaurants as second chef.

Hungry for another adventure, and having an equal love of food and fashion, Maxie moved to New York and worked for CHANEL. After a year she followed her head, heart and stomach, and traded in her power suit for a chef jacket to attended The International Culinary Center where she obtained her diploma in Classic Culinary Arts.

Maxine's favourite things include ricotta, crab, sequins, running, aniseed and cured meats.

Artist Biographies

Adam Oehlers
adamoehlers.com

Adam has always loved getting lost in a story. He uses his illustration work and sculpture to build up a world that others can lose themselves in. Adam tries to include a sense of nostalgia in all of his work, wanting the viewer to be transported back to a time when they were a child. The themes in his stories are often simple, yet seem far from simple to the character experiencing them. Adam enjoys putting an ordinary character in an extraordinary situation or showing an extraordinary character experiencing something ordinary. His stories are often dark and gloomy, but it is the little elements of hope within these stories that capture his imagination.

Adel Cox
departmentdelux.com

For the past fifteen years Adel has been a dedicated designer and illustrator. After completing several fine art courses and a Bachelor of Arts in Animation, she found herself thrust into the world of advertising. Adel has created 'look and feel' campaigns for retail stores and boutique clients, including some of Brisbane's largest design firms. Adel's work is mostly print-based, and she likes to draw things by hand.

Alexandra Emmons
alexandraemmons.tumblr.com

Alexandra Emmons was born and raised in Los Gatos, California. She attended Boston University earning a BFA in Painting, with minors in Printmaking and Art History. She currently lives and works in New York.

Archie Lee Coates

Archie Lee Coates IV was born on a beach and raised in America. He lives a strange and adventurous life with Emily, his beautiful bride, and Akiva, his cat. Archie spends most of his time at PlayLab Inc. in Brooklyn, New York, where he and Jeff Franklin, his best friend, make what they want. This includes a floating pool in Manhattan's East River, an exhibition in Stockholm involving magnification, and a hideout in the woods north of New York City.

Arran Gregory
arrangregory.com

Arran Gregory is a London-based illustrator and sculptor. Having graduated from Chelsea College of Art and Design in 2009, he has since exhibited in numerous exhibitions around the capital and has had successful solo shows.

He works freelance from his studio in the woods and is inspired by all things nature-esque. Arran's work is graphically playful, balancing the maximal with the minimal.

Beastman
beastman.com.au

Beastman is an artist based in Sydney. Influenced by the beauty and symbolism behind nature's repetitive geometric patterns and organic lines, Beastman's tightly detailed, often symmetrical paintings depict a parallel world of hope and survival inhabited by his beastlike, yet beautiful and emotive characters. One of the most distinctive and prolific emerging artists in Australia, and founder and editor of the online art publication [weAREtheIMAGEmakers], Beastman has exhibited extensively throughout Australia and overseas. Beastman was recently named Best Artist at the 2010 Sydney Music, Arts & Culture (SMAC) Awards and his large public mural aerosol works can be found all over Australia and in London, Berlin and New York.

Belinda Suzette
belindasuzette.com

Belinda is a cross-disciplinary folk artist, illustrator and designer living in Melbourne. Inspired by culture and celebration, Belinda's work covers a range of styles in both digital and traditional mediums. Her confident use of colour and her figurative approach conjure memories of childhood, paying homage to the illustrative artists and designers of the 1960s and 1970s with a contemporary sophistication. For an assignment once, as a poor art student, she created a series of drawings entitled 'Starving Artist', made from condiments on rice paper, which she then baked.

Benjamin Clarke

Benjamin J. Clarke develops decadent narratives in his drawing and paintings. Set in surreal lands, Clarke's subjects oscillate between contemporary characters and representations of mythological creatures. Somewhat contorted, his subjects appear to self-deprecate themselves — his motley crew is controlled by a whimsical palette of concentrated watercolour and contours of ink.

In 2009, Clarke graduated from Pratt Institute, Brooklyn, receiving a BFA in Communications Design (majoring in Illustration). He has exhibited in a number of galleries and contributed to commercial artworks. His studio is located at Fowler Arts Collective in Brooklyn.

Billie Justice Thomson
billiejusticethomson.com

After studying Visual Arts for four years at the South Australian School of Art, Billie decided to concentrate wholeheartedly on her painting. Billie connects her practice with a sense of home and the kitchen, trusting her taste and instincts for painting. Billie Justice Thomson's work reflects her obsession with kitsch, nostalgic and iconic food imagery. Her paintings on glass and perspex reference old shop windows or displays with symbols of domestic simplicity.

Camilla Jones
Camilla is a graduate of the University of the West of England, Bristol, in Drawing and Applied Arts. Her time there gave her the freedom to experiment extensively with pattern making, fabric design and wallpapers — these are her areas of expertise. Camilla's recent work focussed on sustainability — a body of work that utilised visual aids, such as distinct patterns to emphasise environmental responsibilities. She is hoping to develop these patterns and release them into the homes of people who wish to live more sustainably.

Clay Hickson
clayhickson.com
Clay Hickson is a Californian-born, Chicago-based printmaker and freelance illustrator. The son of a 1970s airbrush pioneer and a Midwestern art therapist, Hickson is influenced by 1960s psychedelia and 1980s postmodern design. When he is not busy drawing, he is on a bi-coastal, trans-national search for the perfect slice.

Daniel O'Toole
earstotheground.net
Sydney-born painter Daniel O'Toole, also known as 'Ears', works on the streets and in the studio with a loose, abstract portrait style that plays with lyrical line work and bold colours.

Having studied at the National Art School, Daniel has pushed in an anti-institutional direction, building a body of work that combines his learnings from a street art background with an undercurrent of traditionalism, and demonstrates an ability to balance his influences in a focussed effort. His work is inspired and driven by music, life and the city.

David Williams
www.gilimbaa.com.au
David first picked up a paintbrush during his studies at university. After several successful exhibitions, David began to experiment with merging traditional art and digital graphic design techniques and in 2008 started to explore the way Indigenous art and design could be used in modern communication. This led to the formation of Gilimbaa, an Indigenous creative agency based in Brisbane.

'As an Aboriginal man, I share my knowledge of culture through dialogue and practice. This is Indigenous Australia in the 21st century, and we communicate culture through a variety of mediums.'

Drew Funk
drewfunk.com
Born in Malaysia, Drew Funk resides in Melbourne and can usually be found creating at Blender Studios. As well as on the streets, Drew has exhibited nationally and internationally. Through solo and group shows and a prolific street art reputation, Drew has established himself as a key player in the street and fine art worlds. Graduating with a Bachelor of Multimedia and Design from RMIT University, Drew's design background is evident through his illustrative clean style of working, inspired by a fascination with his cultural heritage and the continual influences of nostalgia and the art of city streets.

Emico Isobe
flickr.com/people/emi_i
Emico was born in Japan and lives in Tokyo. She took lessons of illustration at a culture centre once a week for three years and has been creating artworks since 2008. Emico works in an office during the day and paints pictures at night. In the future, she would like to act as an artist all day.

Emily Devers
daily-make.com
MIMI's work appears in many forms, including installation, illustration, painting and interactive live works. MIMI lives to create, collaborate and co-exist with those who care about quality and soul. The common thread of her work seeks to explore and understand ideas of consciousness, balance and spiritual and ethical relationships.

Erin Lightfoot
erinlightfoot.com
A print, pattern and porcelain jewellery maker, Erin is based in Brisbane. She has a part degree in graphic design and a full degree in fashion. She is a colour, collaboration, and cooking enthusiast.

Erin Smith
www.erinsmith.com.au
Erin Smith is a fine artist and illustrator who has recently returned to Queensland after obtaining a Bachelor of Design Arts in Melbourne. Her best-known works are the meticulous compositions dreamed up by the artist and built using only letters. Erin's work has been exhibited both nationally and internationally.

Fanny Dolhain
www.fanni.fr
Fanny Dolhain is a French graphic designer, illustrator and jewellery designer. She describes herself as a visual storyteller. Fanny graduated with a BA in Illustration and Graphic Design from LISAA, Paris and also has an MA in graphic design from Chelsea College of Arts and Design, London. Fanny has worked at a London design agency and set up a jewellery brand F comme. She is currently freelancing in Paris.

Felicity Harrold
Felicity spends her time drawing, baking, watching films and making lists of things she wants to do and be and change. She is yet to learn French, master the fiddle or visit Kentucky. She needs to fall in love ... but clean her room first.

Femke de Jong
femillustration.com
Femke's work focuses on creating images with a curious and whimsical feel. By juxtaposing and layering image and context digitally and by hand, she designs surreal characters and landscapes. Femke gets her ideas through observation, research and experimentation with materials and techniques. Femke's work evolves around her fascination with the relationship between man and machine, often customizing existing objects by 're-appropriating' them with mechanical and nostalgic elements.

Funny Banana
funnybanana.co.uk
Victor was born in Lisbon's oldest district, Alfama, Portugal. He migrated with his family to England in 1993. He is a father of four and grandfather of two. As if that doesn't keep him busy enough, in his spare time he works alongside his wife of many decades in their family-run business. He is a concierge by vocation, but has always had a passion for self-taught graphic design. He recently discovered the magic of embroidery design and has taken it to heart. He never turns down a challenge and strongly believes everything can translate into embroidery.

Gabrielle Herzog
gabrieleherzog.com
Gabriele Herzog is a freelance illustrator and artist who lives and works in London. Gabrielle grew up in Basel, Switzerland, where she got her BA at the Schule für Gestaltung Basel. She moved to London in 2009 and later graduated from the University of Arts London (Camberwell College of Arts) with an MA in Illustration. Selected clients include, Paul Smith, AllCity and Frank.

HAW
hellohaw.com
Haw is a Hong Kong–Australian illustrator and designer living in outback Australia creating digital interactive comics. He is formally trained in design, illustration and three-dimensional design and has produced a diverse body of work over the past decade. These range from commissioned murals, furniture design, fashion, customised bike, skate and snowboard art, illustration and comics. His philosophy is: 'keep it simple, keep it awesome.'

Hiyato Yoshinari
Hiyato was born in Tokyo in the late 1970s.
He paints, draws and makes collages. His
influences come from op-shops, roadside
collections and art that is reminiscent of his
own cultural background, such as manga and
animation. Hiyato is also influenced by a variety
of music, pop art, street art and subcultures.

Helen Schroeder
lindenleaf.etsy.com
Helen Schroeder was born and raised in
Minneapolis, but now calls Boston home. She
is particularly interested in the transformative
power of art at an individual and community
level, and currently coordinates the art program
at a local homeless shelter. She is also the artist
behind Linden Leaf designs, a collection of
colourful greeting cards and prints celebrating
her hometown pride. In her spare time, you
can find her travelling, digging around in her
community garden plot or cooking pesto pasta
for people she loves.

Hilde Thomsen
hildethomsen.com
Hilde is a Melbourne-based illustrator and artist
from the fjords of Norway. Her work tells a
story, often referencing people's body language
and facial expressions, to communicate a mood
or a narrative. Her work is satirical and full of
subtle humour. An interest in psychology,
group dynamics and people in general has led
her towards editorial and social commentary
illustration.

Inés Inglesias
pintaycolorea.es
A versatile and creative artist, Inés participates
in national and international festivals and
events such as Sonar in Barcelona, Biennale
di Venezia, Torino Film Festival, Amore in Rome
and Cinetrip in Budapest, to name a few.
    Her work reflects her knowledge and
personality as a multimedia artist, able to
express herself through the various languages
of illustration, graphic design, silkscreen, 3D
and video to create colourful performances.

Jack Douglas
jdouglasart.blogspot.com
Heralding from the outer eastern suburbs of
Melbourne, Jack Douglas grew up during a
time when the mullet and happy pants were
still in fashion. Propelled by this awesomeness,
he drew great influence from Hanna-Barbera,
Looney Tunes, tattoo flash, skateboard graphics,
comics and the artwork of Salvador Dali and
MC Escher. During his teens he discovered
graffiti art and pop surrealism. His images are
often grotesque, shining a spotlight on those
who dwell on the outskirts of our society and
the darkly humorous situations they land
themselves in.

Jade Borjesson
colourjade.com
Jade is based in Melbourne and has a long
love for colour pencils and the intricate detail
of nature. She is currently working on a series
exploring the romance of illusion in both
women and the natural world. Jade has been
commissioned for portraits and involved closely
in album art design. 'I am inspired by nature
and the unique ways in which we perceive our
world. I aspire to create art that slowly reveals
itself as the viewer and artwork meet.'

James Kape
jameskape.com
omsestudio.com
Heralding from Sydney, James Kape is a New
York-based designer. He focuses primarily on
branding, print and web design and has been
featured in a number of blogs and publications.
James is inspired by refined design, typography
and photography. He approaches each project
with interest and enthusiasm, striving to
create something both visually effective and
appropriate for its intended audience.

Jen Hillhouse
jenniferhillhouse.tumblr.com
Jennifer Hillhouse is a graphic designer and
illustrator working in Brisbane. The world and
people around her influence a lot of her design
and illustration style. She enjoys creating
unusual landscapes and animals from her
collection of photographs, textures and furs.
Jennifer likes animals (especially sausage dogs
and moose), moustaches, scarves, playing
violin, indoor soccer and spending time with
her friends and family.

James Dodd
james-dodd.com
James Dodd's work traverses the boundaries
between visual street culture, alternative use
of urban space and existing gallery conventions.
Primarily, his work revolves around the use of
found text, such as graffiti.
    Dodd principally works as a painter,
however he often experiments with the
construction of objects to paint on for the
purpose of large-scale installations. James has
recently completed a Masters of Visual Arts
by Research at the South Australian School
of Art.

Jo Pole
jopole.com
Jo pole is a self-taught illustrator from
Queensland Australia. Jo has recently
returned from three years in Melbourne, one
of Australia's most vibrant creative hubs. Jo's
highly detailed illustrations are mostly inspired
by pop culture and have been exhibited in
Brisbane, Melbourne, Hong Kong and
New York.

Joe Baker
bakedlab.com
Born in a city, then raised in the sticks in central
Queensland, Australia, Joe has always drawn
influence from the experience of growing
up in a small town, creating work based on
witnessing quiet, mundane and repetitive
aspects of everyday life and twisting them into
obscure fantasy. Almost like trying to recreate
a daydream. Joe plays with this concept
through a series of different media experiments,
represented in both still and animated forms.

Josh Rufford
ruffoart.com
Josh is a Brisbane-based graphic artist, with
a strong focus on drawing while maintaining
a significant multiple-medium practice. He
likes to draw, paint and animate using pens,
ink, acrylic, watercolours and any kind of
found objects to create interesting visual
compositions. He works as a graphic designer
by day and freelance illustrator and animator
by night. He is also one half of the dynamic
duo known as Ruffbat Creative, with his wife
Rhiannon McLay.

Kai Nødland
kainodland.com
Born and raised in Norway, Kai now works and
lives in London, where people often seem to
mistake him for a German or South African.

Katie Willmet
'I'd like to sit for a while
drink tea and hear your stories
of things you did as a child
I'd like to see your drawings
and admire your fingers and hair
make cheese and pickle sandwiches
and wonder how you're feeling
when nobody is near.'

King Adz
100proof.tv
King Adz is an author and creative director who
specialises in the creation and documentation
of Youth Culture. He has travelled constantly
for the past fifteen years, examining global
youth talent and subcultures. He has been
lucky enough to work with some of the most
influential and interesting people around.

Kitty Horton
kittyhorton.com.au
Kitty Horton is a Brisbane-based artist. She
has exhibited in solo shows in Melbourne and
Sydney. Her chosen medium is acrylic on wood,
ink and soft sculpture toys. Kitty uses her art to
explore concepts, ages and cultures. Through
her work she has examined semiotics, historical
figures, anatomy and modern Japanese culture.

Kirsten Williamson

Kirsten Williamson is an aspiring fashion designer and illustrator, studying a Bachelor of Fine Arts (Fashion) at QUT, Brisbane. Her artistic style is realism and she works predominantly in graphite, watercolour, biros and pretty much anything she can find on the desk. She also really likes drawing frangipanis.

Liam Stevens
liamstevens.com

Liam Stevens is an image maker and designer based in London. He favours simple materials enabling him to craft his work through expressive lines or graphic shapes and is particularly fond of his Pentel 0.7mm mechanical pencil, coloured paper stash and scalpel. Liam co-formed MakeMakeStudio with Chris Tozer as an outlet to motion experimentation and animation.

Liam has work held in the Kanazawa 21st Century Museum of Art's permanent collection in Japan. His clients include Anya Hindmarch, New Statesman, The Ride Journal, Eye Spy Gallery, Booklet Tokyo, Conde Nast, The Rug Company, Little Otsu and My Robot Friend.

Lucy James
lucyjames.net

Armed with a medical scalpel and a keen eye, Lucy harvests images from discarded and forgotten books and melds them into carefully composed hybrids of form and meaning. Touching on issues of inherited folklore, the commodification of pets and the exploitation of natural resources, Lucy's work appears playful and visually dynamic, while allowing for deeper interpretative meaning. Lucy has studied Visual Arts, Fashion and Textiles and most recently completed her Honours degree in Fine Art in 2009. Since then, she has exhibited nationally and internationally, and at times dips her toes into the land of illustration and design.

Luke Brown
lukebrown.com.au

Luke produces work across an array of disciplines, including art direction, design and custom typography for clients in Australia and internationally. Luke brings a wealth of experience and energy to each project, working for clients across a range of industries, including music, editorial, fashion, exhibition, advertising, branding and consulting.

Max Berry
idlepassage.blogspot.com

Max Berry's work creates a world where every object has a life of its own, a daydream land where houses talk to clouds and characters float playfully in abstracted space. Max is interested in imaginary worlds where his characters can exist in a heightened state of duality, exploring obscure lore and strange, unknown lands. His characters appear in many forms, as paste-ups, stickers, on canvas, walls, in live painting sessions and cardboard busking. In addition to his work with Oh Really, Max has become part of the cultural landscape of inner Sydney.

Mark Lazenby
marklazenby.co.uk

Mark's work is all collage and montage. He has been working as a collage artist, illustrator and graphic designer for over fifteen years, exhibiting around the world. He has had work published by Penguin, in 'Time', 'The New York Times' and 'Vogue', to name a few.

'Mark is a very good collagist in the best tradition of collage making, via Kurt Schwitters and Joseph Cornell. What makes him even more interesting though, is an interest in, and a beautiful use of typography in his work. I am a fan, and owner of a collage by him.' — Sir Peter Blake.

Mumptown
mumptown.co.uk

We Mumps from Mumptown are Ceri and Oliver. Our world is made up of funny and weird characters. We like cats, pencils, toys, books, biscuits, beats, slow lorises, Gucci Mane, sneakers, tea and cake, Totoro, Posca pens, Supreme, gangsta rap, bikes, Ting, bobble hats, 'Adventure Time' and Michael Scott.

Naomi Lees-Maiberg
etsy.com/shop/workingwoman

'I always wanted to grow and nurture things. With my kids all grown up and out of the house, I moved outside. Forty years after Woodstock I'm back in the garden. With only a few months in which I can grow things in Maine, it's a tough juggle between what I want to do and what I really want to do. When I am on my knees weeding the radishes and talking to the tomatoes, my studio might as well be in Canada. It's a fight. Sometimes I lose, and sometimes I win. But it feels like a win-win to me. I have always drawn and painted and written about fruits and vegetables. Nothing gets lost when you grow, paint and eat them. I didn't intend to, but I'm being good to myself and the planet.'

Nadine Sawyer
nadinesawyer.com

Diversity is the word that best describes Nadine's art practice. Nadine is predominantly a painter of both figurative and abstract works that she sells and exhibits in interior stores, galleries and online. She has developed a collection of tea towels, greeting cards and linen prints using her images, which have a joyful, poetic, humorous and uplifting aesthetic.

Nadine is passionate about her Installation work called 'Beautiful Object Poetry' — installations are made with found objects, fresh fruit, vegetables and flowers.

Nadine studied at RMIT and Monash in Melbourne and then lived and exhibited in the US and Japan and is now based on the Sunshine Coast, Australia.

Numskull
funskull.com

Numskull is an Australian-based artist working as a painter, illustrator and decorator. He has spent a good part of his life fascinated and engrossed in the graffiti and street art movements, and has become a prominent name both inside galleries and on outside walls. Working on both canvas and small to large outdoor murals, his work uses pop iconography, typography, signage and nostalgic ideas to convey bold images of an other-worldy nature. His style and practice has evolved through meeting people and gaining knowledge from the graffiti and street art communities. He has shown in galleries, painted walls and sold paintings in London, Singapore, Amsterdam, Hong Kong, Tokyo, Paris and Australia.

Pamela Oberman

White kanaka. PNG dweller. Mother of two seriously interesting cats (she refers to her children as cats!). Born in Longreach. Raised in a cooly in PNG. Met deep, artistic hubby in Sydney (linked to Thompson tribe some four decades ago). Get in touch with Pamela if you are looking for a marriage celebrant for the bohemian couple, some cool art to hang on your walls, some serious interior decorating solutions or for some real-life musicians for your next party.

Rachael Bartram
thisartstead.blogspot.com

During her studies at QCA, Brisbane, Rachael worked with concepts relating to visual narrative, the silhouette image, family history and the dream state. During this time she began collecting small clusters of older books and magazines. As her collection grew, Rachael became more enthralled in the process of cutting and extracting images and text from the pages. Drawing parallels with collage, she loves the process of cooking — melding together contrasting flavours, textures, tools and methodologies. In the future, Rachael hopes to perfect hollandaise sauce, but for now, she's mastered a supple Spanish mousse.

Rosalind Monks
rosalindmonks.com

Rosalind is a freelance illustrator based in the UK. Born and raised in Switzerland, her love and fascination for the natural world is a huge influence in her drawing. Her background and interest in fashion and textiles also plays an important role in informing the patterns she uses and creates within her work.

Rhiannon McLay
rhiannonmclay.com

Rhiannon is a Brisbane-based freelance illustrator and designer who works primarily in watercolour. Rhiannon graduated with a Bachelor of Visual Art (Illustration major) from the Queensland College of Art in 2003, and with a Masters in Digital Design (Web Screen Specialisation) in 2009. She has worked as a graphic designer in the signage industry, illustrated five published children's books and had her artwork exhibited locally. Rhiannon has an infatuation with coloured pencils, tomatoes and bees, and finds great solace in fresh paint.

Riki Salam
gilimbaa.com.au

Continuing to explore the beauty of art, design and storytelling in the Indigenous space, Riki has developed a series of paintings that speak of belonging, heritage, identity and the triumph of the human spirit. Riki is based in Brisbane and works at indigenous creative agency, Gilimbaa.

RYOONO
ryoono.com

RYOONO is a graphic artist based in Tokyo, Japan. He creates colourful graphics and murals, and collaborates on various projects within the apparel and restaurant industries.

Sarah Dennis
sarah-dennis.co.uk

Sarah's work invokes a tale of innocence with a contemporary feel. Her artwork is inspired by nature, old books, friends and fancy dress. Her artwork is created from line drawings and collages together with an assortment of textures. As well as her illustrations, Sarah has also made a name with her handcrafted felt characters, children's book, zines and badges, which are available from her online shop.

Seamus Ashley
seamusandsons.com

Seamus is a Melbourne-based designer and web developer. After completing a Bachelor of Design (Visual Communication) at Monash University, Seamus established his own business Seamus & Sons. When Seamus isn't working on his RSI, he can often be found in his most sacred of places, the kitchen, where his love of cooking and consumption of delicious liqueurs from around the world, help him not think about his aforementioned condition.

'Tell me what you eat and I'll tell you what you are,' is a quote Seamus hopes one day to use at an inappropriate moment.

Simon MacEwan
simon-macewan.blogspot.com

Simon studied a Diploma of Visual Art and a Bachelor of Fine Art in sculpture at RMIT. Since graduating in 2002, he has been a practising artist working in sculpture, drawing, animation and installation, and exhibiting at galleries. Simon is the former deputy director of Seventh Gallery in Fitzroy (2006–2008), and former Curator of First Site RMIT Union Gallery (2007–2008). In 2004, Simon began the Lost in The Woods jewellery label and is currently working as an artist, jewellery designer and maker, illustrator and welder.

Tai Snaith
taisnaith.com

Tai Snaith has a multifaceted practice working as an independent artist, curator, producer and writer. She draws and paints on paper, on the street and recently inside restaurants and houses. Honesty, absurdity and animism heavily influence her artwork and ideas alongside a recurring focus on collaboration and experimentation. Using collage and drawing, Snaith often explores inner thoughts, spiritual beliefs and apocalyptic visions of the greater animal kingdom. She moonlights as a cattle judge and her parents breed Warialda Belted Galloway cattle. She has a little boy called Leo, a cat called Clive and a horse called Nazif.

Teebs
mtendere.tumblr.com

Teebs developed his artistry right outside Los Angeles' county line and just south of the Orange County beach community. A skateboard injury sidelined Teebs, which led to a concentration on art. Through great focus and vision, he has made a name for himself as a skilled painter. His artwork can be found on canvases of all forms, from walls to record covers, all imbued with vibrant colour, energy, and shape. Teebs is also involved in the world of music making, affiliated with the Brainfeeder label and My Hollow Drum collective.

Thembi Hanify
thembihanify.com

Thembi Hanify is a graphic designer living and working in New York City. She grew up in Brisbane and lived in Sydney for six months prior to throwing herself in the deep end of the city that never sleeps. Thembi is fascinated by colour and shape at the most basic and complex levels. She finds herself being drawn to the boundaries of primitive simplicity and kitsch, and finds this the ultimate challenge in approaching and executing projects in a unique way. Thembi currently works for a digital studio with high-profile fashion clients. In her spare time she designs typefaces and dabbles in inventive pescetarian cooking.

Trent Evans
passportal.com.au

Trent Evans is a Sydney-based artist and designer and founder of PASS-PORT, a boutique skateboarding and apparel label.

Vexta
vexta.com.au

Vexta is an artist from Australia. She was born in Sydney but now lives and works in Melbourne. She has been creating street art since 2005 and is most famously known for her stencils and paste-ups, which draw from cultural visual debris, her self-taught aesthetic and an ongoing exploration of painting and printmaking. Her neon-drenched images are influenced by a personal symbolism and a greater urban mythology, which connect the dots between street rallies and galleries, acute social commentary and aching beauty.

Her work has been shown in exhibitions across Australia and internationally. She likes to make things with paintbrushes, spray paint and pens, and can be found biking through the city late at night listening to beautiful songs about the end of the world.

Victoria Topping
victoriatopping.com

Victoria works as a freelance illustrator and graphic designer in Bristol. She likes to spend her days and most nights in her Stokes Croft studio glued to her computer creating new images. She's heavily influenced by the disco 12" sleeves in her record box as well as music in general. She inherited her love of patterns from her mother, who is a wallpaper historian and printer. Victoria works alongside her mother, restoring and reproducing old wallpapers, whilst creating her own range called 'exotica'. As a result, she has a huge collection of wallpapers that she uses in her work. In her spare time, Victoria scours vintage and charity shops for fabrics she can use, as well as creating her own with whatever she finds.

Warren Handley
ten-p-bag.blogspot.com

Warren Handley migrated to Australia from the southeast of England in 2005 and has been living in Brisbane ever since. He studied a Bachelor of Visual Media, majoring in Fine Art, at Griffith University and has since gone on to complete Honours. Believing that creativity should not be limited to the use of a single medium, Warren's practice is as varied as his interests. From mixed media assemblages to the making of visuals for Brisbane's underground club nights, Warren likes to keep his creative fingers in many delicious pies!

First and foremost, a giant thank you to all the artists who have contributed to the book – their talent and enthusiasm has been a massively inspirational and rewarding part of this project.

Of course a huge thanks to our parents for their love and support – mum's recipe creativity and dad's wisdom and appetite have made this book possible. Thanks to Sean, Georgie's husband, for his unconditional patience and love for all three of us.

We're ever grateful to our legion of amazing friends for their company, laughs and taste-testing. Special shout-outs need to go to good friend and photographer Megan Cullen for her inspiration and dancefloor heat, and Lauren Zanetti for her inimitable business nous. Thanks also to Alex Adsett and King Adz for their guidance and advice.

Lastly, a big thank you to the team at Murdoch Books – Sally, Alice, Mary-Jayne, Shannon, our patient editors Jacqueline and Michelle, editorial manager Livia and designer Miriam – for supporting the project in its early days and allowing us to share our food with more people than we'd ever hoped.

Index

Published in 2013 by Murdoch Books Pty Limited

Murdoch Books Australia
83 Alexander Street
Crows Nest NSW 2056
Phone: +61 (0) 2 8425 0100
Fax: +61 (0) 2 9906 2218
www.murdochbooks.com.au
info@murdochbooks.com.au

Murdoch Books UK Limited
Erico House, 6th Floor
93–99 Upper Richmond Road
Putney, London SW15 2TG
Phone: +44 (0) 20 8785 5995
Fax: +44 (0) 20 8785 5985
www.murdochbooks.co.uk
info@murdochbooks.co.uk

For Corporate Orders & Custom Publishing contact Noel Hammond,
National Business Development Manager Murdoch Books Australia

Publisher: Sally Webb
Designer: Miriam Steenhauer
Project Managers: Livia Caiazzo, Alice Grundy
Editor: Jacqueline Blanchard
Food Editor: Michelle Earl
Production Manager: Karen Small

Text © Jessica, Maxine and Georgie Thompson
The moral rights of the authors have been asserted.
Design © Murdoch Books Pty Limited 2013
Front cover art by Lucy James
Back cover art by Fanny Dolhain

A cataloguing-in-publication entry is available from the catalogue of the National Library
of Australia at www.nla.gov.au.

A catalogue record for this book is available from the British Library.

Printed by 1010 Printing International Limited, China

IMPORTANT: Those who might be at risk from the effects of salmonella poisoning (the elderly,
pregnant women, young children and those suffering from immune deficiency diseases) should
consult their doctor with any concerns about eating raw eggs.

OVEN GUIDE: You may find cooking times vary depending on the oven you are using.
For fan-forced ovens, as a general rule, set the oven temperature to 20°C (35°F) lower than
indicated in the recipe.

We have used 20 ml (4 teaspoon) tablespoon measures. If you are using a 15 ml (3 teaspoon)
tablespoon add an extra teaspoon of the ingredient for each tablespoon specified.